SEEING THE RAVEN

Also by Peter M. Leschak

Letters from Side Lake

The Bear Guardian

Bumming with the Furies

Hellroaring

SEEING THE RAVEN

A NARRATIVE OF RENEWAL

PETER M. LESCHAK

University of Minnesota Press
Minneapolis / London

Portions of this book, in altered form, were first published in *Mpls.-St. Paul Magazine*, *Minnesota Monthly*, the *New North Times*, Minneapolis *Star Tribune Sunday Magazine*, the *Minnesota Volunteer*, the *Saint Paul Pioneer Press Dispatch*, *Buzzworm*, *Astronomy*, *Lake Superior Magazine*, *Farm Family America*, the *Window*, *Country Journal*, *Twin Cities Reader*, and *Fine Gardening*.

Grateful acknowledgment is made for permission to reprint from the following: Stephen Vincent Benét, "American Names," in *Selected Works of Stephen Vincent Benét*, copyright 1927 by Stephen Vincent Benét, copyright renewed 1955 by Thomas C. Benét, Stephanie B. Mahin, and Rachel Carr Benét, reprinted by permission of Brandt & Brandt, Literary Agents, Inc.; William Butler Yeats, "Anashuya and Vijaya," in *The Poems of W. B. Yeats: A New Edition*, edited by Richard J. Finneran (New York: Macmillan, 1983), by permission of Macmillan; Paul Simon, "The Sound of Silence," copyright 1964, copyright renewed by Paul Simon, used by permission of the publisher; Dylan Thomas, "The Force That Through the Green Fuse Drives the Flower," in *Poems of Dylan Thomas*, copyright 1939 by New Directions Publishing Corporation, reprinted by permission of New Directions Publishing Corporation and David Higham Associates. The publishers ask copyright holders to contact them if permission has inadvertently not been sought or if proper acknowledgment has not been made.

Published by the University of Minnesota Press
2037 University Avenue Southeast
Minneapolis, MN 55455-3092

Printed in the United States of America on acid-free paper

Library of Congress Cataloging-in-Publication Data

Leschak, Peter M., 1951–
Seeing the raven : a narrative of renewal / Peter M. Leschak.
p. cm.
ISBN 0-8166-2429-1
1. Minnesota—Description and travel. 2. Minnesota—Social life and customs. I. Title.
F610.L495 1994
977.6—dc20   93-27943

The University of Minnesota is an
equal-opportunity educator and employer.

Flashes the fire of sadness, for they see
The icicles that famish all the north,
Where men lie frozen in the glimmering snow;
And in the flaming forests cower the lion
And lioness, with all their whimpering cubs;
And, ever pacing on the verge of things,
The phantom, Beauty, in a mist of tears;
While we alone have round us woven woods,
And feel the softness of each other's hand . . .

W. B. Yeats

The University of Minnesota Press gratefully acknowledges
assistance provided for the publication of this volume by the
John K. and Elsie Lampert Fesler Fund.

Contents

A u t h o r ' s   N o t e

The person called "Mal" in this book is real, and his experiences in Vietnam are all true, but his name and the details of his present life have been changed to protect his privacy. "Duke," "Sandy," and "Milt" are also pseudonyms.

My reference for many of the Native American stories and myths presented in this book was *American Indian Myths and Legends,* edited by Richard Erdoes and Alfonso Ortiz, published by Pantheon. It's an excellent book and I highly recommend it.

A c k n o w l e d g m e n t s

Thanks to Lisa Freeman of the University of Minnesota Press;
the magazine editors who gave some of this material its first chance,
especially Loree Miltich, Greg Breining, Glen Warchol, and Doug Hanson;
and Deborah Vajda for her perceptive editing of the manuscript.

My name is Windigo, and I am a hunter. I roam the woods alone like a wolf cast from the pack. I relish bitter January nights, when the moon rides high and snow glitters like the starscape overhead. On such nights I own the dark forest and frozen rivers. I'm emperor of the deer in their yards, chief of the bears in their dens. I'm lord of the fish under the ice and ruler of the beaver in its lodge. My authority is unchallenged because no one knows it exists. I consider the world my realm, and there are no revolutions. My power is secret and therefore absolute. My judgments are silent and therefore never disputed. I'm content to govern on winter nights. As my breath rises to the stars on the northwest wind, I'm satisfied to leave no pattern of tracks across a frozen sky. I'm happy to listen to owls and wolves calling my name. They know it well.

But winters pass, and others arrive to claim the wild. Quiet winter twilights yield to fertile clamorings of spring. I have little sway over tadpoles, eggs, and tender young shoots. The renewal of April knows no sovereign. But as the setting sun tracks northward, I begin my yearly hunt. I'm not a hunter of moose or a forager of rabbits. I'm a hunter of men, and they fear me. They do not know my name. They imagine that owls are calling only for their mates. They are sure wolves howl merely among

themselves. Such is the nature of men. But if they believe
the owls and wolves are only conversing, then why do
men shiver to hear it? Why do they toss in the night with
the moon in their faces? Perhaps they've glimpsed me
over a distant ridge, briefly silhouetted by the setting
sun.

My name is Windigo, and I know the trees. When they
die their limbs shrivel into brittle sticks. The aspen and
birch, the pine and fir—they are all the same to me. I've
wandered for centuries, and I'm older than many trees.
I've seen them age into deadfalls. I've seen them uproot-
ed by wind and eaten by ants. I've seen them consumed
by fire and split by lightning. I understand that sky is
more potent than forest. The sky breeds wind and is
adorned with changeless stars. But I do not revere the
heavens. Even mere rocks endure the seasons. I am
Windigo, and I offer wings to what is invisible.

Even I was once young. Once the moss was a cushion
and balsam pitch like incense. The lakes were cool foun-
tains, the snow a carpet of crystal. The forest was a mother, a nurse, a poetess. The river flats were choked with
wild rice, and blueberries filled the meadows. Deer were
fat, and grouse were trusting. But with time there were
other visions. The forest is also a sorceress. Her spells are
lavished on all—on butcher and healer alike. She will
easily deal death to both, and stars will take no notice.

So I hunt men—not for their blood, but for their souls.
I track the spoor of their spirits and take them alive. I
want their minds, I want their fear. The earth will have
their bodies one day—perhaps to nourish trees. But I
wish to feed the night wind that moans among the pines.

It's enough that the people see me or hear me. If they look and listen, I have their heart; I leave the grasping to water, sky, or stone.

I am Windigo, and I make a human believe:

They will come for me one day. Out of the west, at night. The south wind that brought three inches of new snow will be quartering to the north. The moon will be nearly full, two days short, sailing through ragged, clearing clouds. Pine boughs will be laden with snow, bending under the weight. The bare branches of the aspens will be frosted, glinting in moonlight. Wind, but no sound—no leaves to shake and dance, and fir needles, locked up in winter, will not whisper.

From across a frozen lake, out where ancient air lingers amid the spruce, will come the first warning. I'll be surprised it has arrived so soon, though it was assured from the beginning. A sentinel sunk in memory, in a misty region where matter shades into mind, has known all along. Still, why *this* night? Couldn't it wait another month? Another year? Another decade? Who will begrudge me time? What is ten years to the moon?

But the warning will come. The signal will be a song; a melody borne on air and mingled with the vibrations of the world. The notes will be distinct—like a sharp crack on a January night. Was that the ice sheet, or the shout of a frostbitten birch?

At first the song will sound human. There will be a spectral, flowing chant, and yes, the beat of drums. There are grandfathers out there, the phantoms of hunters and medicine men. They lived with this forest, entwined in cycles with pike, caribou, and rice. They watched the long winters pass, and saw Manitou in the leaping shadows of their lodges. He filled the sky, a great spirit with wind for breath. He sent the northern lights to haunt the silent dark. *"Jee' byug neemeid' dewaud,"* said the Ojibwe—"dancing ghosts."

But the drums will fade. Was it my heartbeat? The dancers will lie down, the warriors will not leap. The chant is a token, a whiff of smoke on the breeze. I am certain that they have gone on before: "I shall not be there. I shall rise and pass. Bury my heart at Wounded Knee."*

After the warning, I'll face the wind. With its cold breath on my cheeks I'll gaze at the stars, prepared. There are wolves out there, a few hunters who sing in the forest. There were many once, but they were hated and could not survive. Some still sing, and I'll hear them again this night. They will begin suddenly, the howls rising up from nothing into a tremulous wave. I'll grin, and my ears will tingle—as sensitive as morning pools. I will listen on the shore of the ice field, brimming with wolf song; not fearing, only feeling. It's in the blood. I, too, must die.

And when the final howl trails off into silence, lost in old spruce air, I will lie down in snow. There will be drumming again—the slowing beat of my heart. I will not rise to the drum. I will not dance. As my heartbeat grows faint and erratic, sounding the last warning, they will come.

Out of the sky they will circle and swoop, watching me. It will be dawn, at the last moments of darkness,

*American Names, *stanza 7, Stephen Vincent Benét* (1927)

when they will glide to earth and begin my passage. They will be sure that I am transformed. Do you see them? The ravens?

But I will not be there.

1

WOLF MOON

I t's astonishing that you can live thirty-some years on this planet and hear a common sound for the first time. That's what I thought when I heard the snow. How many times had I been amidst windblown flakes? A thousand? At least. And yet I'd never listened to them.

I was standing on Secret Lake in northeastern Minnesota. A crescent moon was low in the west, seen white and cold through January air. A gusty southwest wind had the sky frothing and seething in transparent celestial surf, and the stars blinked rapidly in the tumult. A pale greenish glow behind the spruce tops to the north heralded a display of aurora borealis.

I was taking in this light show, relishing the pleasant sting of chilly air on my face, when I finally heard the distant crowd. That's what it sounded like—a throng of bustling people from far across a great plaza in some beehive of a city. It was rushing crystals of snow, hissing and tinkling as they swept across the lake and past me into the woods. There was just enough wind to lift the top layer of snow and push it along the surface in waves of jostling, murmuring particles.

I couldn't see them—except as a general vibration in the moonlight. The lake was as turbulent as the sky, and it was easy to imagine it as shadowy water, not snow-blanketed ice. The sound was enthralling—millions of whispering crystals hurrying by. And I'd never heard them before. Strange.

I think part of my fresh awareness was stimulated by the occasion. It was New Year's Day 1990, and before leaving the cabin to muse by the lakeshore, I'd reviewed my journal for 1989, trying to grasp the events of twelve months gone by, noting what had changed, what hadn't. It was beguiling to realize that in the previous 365 days the earth had completed another orbit around the sun, and that together they (and the rest of the solar system) had trekked 377 million miles through a spiral arm of the Milky Way galaxy. Although the lake and I had inadvertently journeyed with them, I didn't feel so well traveled. During the summer I'd gotten as far as Idaho. Mostly we stay put, and this was the twelfth straight winter in the cabin above Secret Lake. That's enough time to know a place well, and the paradoxical danger is that increased familiarity often translates into decreased awareness. The more you experience something, the less you discern it. The software of the mind believes it knows best, and the lake has been noted and catalogued as much as it needs to be. Our minds will lapse comfortably into ripe, stodgy conservatism if we allow them to. It's easy, it's "normal."

Thus, one of the mantras of human discourse is "keep an open mind," and we've been urged by sages to ventilate our intellects—stay fresh, receptive. Those who caution us otherwise usually have ulterior motives. I once sought ill-considered refuge in a fundamentalist Christian sect, and I vividly recall how the minister ordered us to fear and avoid an open mind. He assured the flock that if an opening were there, one of Satan's demons would probably leap in and possess us. (None but the highest-ranking ministers admitted to the vanity of feeling threatened by Satan himself.) Since we had "the truth," there was no need to be curious, questing, open. That's why fundamentalists (including dogmatists in science, politics, and economics) are so intolerant. They know it all, or will very soon, and have essentially stopped thinking. Those who disagree are automatically ignorant or benighted, and therefore inferior. The minister who extolled the virtues of a closed mind was simultaneously strengthening his personal power over those he had convinced. Thomas Jefferson summed it up this way: "If there were no priests, there would be no infidels." The closed mind is furnished in black and white. I once heard someone say, "A mind is like a parachute; it works only when it's open." It seems to me that if demons are in our midst, they certainly appreciate the utter, evil possessiveness of an unopened parachute.

When I was in jump school, I learned about parachute "malfunction." It's a sinister euphemism, and if it's meant to take the edge off "unopened," it fails. I never heard my jump master make the mind-parachute comparison, but he did offer us a proverb of his own. Speaking of a "major malfunction," he said, "Remember, it doesn't hurt till you hit the ground." It was macho fatalism, of course, the kind of rough-edged cuteness favored by drill sergeants, football coaches, and other males who nurture toughness. But there was also a core of pragmatic wisdom: you won't die until impact; the failure of your main chute isn't what kills, or even bruises; you have an option (cut away and deploy your reserve) and are free to exercise that choice for the several seconds before your death is guaranteed. In the oft-quoted bon mot of Yogi Berra, "It ain't over till it's over." There's no point in prematurely writing off life, the jump master was saying; don't kill yourself before the ground does.

A variation of this insight might be "It ain't perceived till it's perceived." Less poetic, but still evocative of the seemingly endless possibilities of experience. After half a lifetime of northern winters it was a delightful revelation to truly hear the collective voice of millions of ice crystals. What else will I learn about snow? How else will I be startled by the "common"?

The shore of Secret Lake has been good to me in this regard. It's a "place of power" where wonderful perceptions are focused and amplified. Eight days after I heard the snow, I went down to the lake to ski in the radiance of the first full moon of the new year. To the Ojibwe this is the Wolf Moon, and it rode high and glossy—nearly at the zenith. It lent color to the shadows of the forest, and the lake was a snowfield of glimmering sparks. It was below zero, and my exhalations formed pleasing white puffs of mist—the breath of life made visible, wafting off to infinity.

The Reverend, our black mongrel dog, had left his warm kitchen rug to join me. He likes trotting ahead as I ski the trail I keep open around the perimeter of the lake. When we reached the snowfield, and I laid my skis in the tracks, he fidgeted and whined in anticipation. Already his snout and whiskers were frosted, and he looked like a cartoon character—Augie Doggie with a cream pie in the face; old snowpuss. I gave him a playful tap on the rump with a ski pole. Then we both froze.

The howling was so loud I flinched. I spun around to face west, fully expecting to see a wolf pack across the lake. That's what I wished—to glimpse black shapes sprinting across the ice in the moonlight. For an instant my heart surged when I imagined it was true. But no, the cluster of shadows on the far shore was only humps of sphagnum. The timberwolves were back in the trees, or perhaps on the neighboring lake. But their baying and wailing charged my body to an electric pitch of acuity. I was hearing the music of wilderness—a song of sinew, blood, and gray fur. If there's a Creator, then this was one of the voices of God.

The Reverend was wired, ears and hackles up. He knew this melody better than I. His cousins were calling, and I envied his direct link to those wild ones. How did this sound in *his* ears? Was he afraid or excited, challenged or warned? What ancestral signals stirred his brain?

The clamor continued for about a minute and then died as abruptly as it had begun. The silence left behind was resonant and rich—suffused with power. I trembled in rapture . . . and yearning. I threw my head back to stare at the moon; I opened my mouth and howled. The dog jerked around, startled. He whined. But as my howl trailed off, he suddenly joined in, and we harmonized—a pack unto ourselves. For a moment it was quiet again, then a lone voice was raised from the west, a single, guttural howl. I laughed aloud. Had we really been answered? I cupped my hands around my mouth and bent back to the moon. Had that light ever been quite so vibrant? Inspired, I reached for all the air my lungs would hold and wailed as intensely as I could. The Reverend joined in.

The lone voice replied immediately. It was magic; I was linked. These were my cousins, too, at least for a little while, and never had I felt as close to the spirit of the wild—enmeshed in the mystery of sentient life. What a privilege to perform in a chorus so ancient and beautiful. I was happy, and I howled again. The Rev declined; he was jumpy now. But the wolf answered me for a third and last time. My fourth howl drifted away into silence.

But it wasn't the end. Several minutes later the entire pack burst into song. They seemed even closer, and my neck tingled. Then far off to the southwest I heard another pack, a second group of wolves singing to their namesake moon. They were barely audible, probably miles away. I pictured them on a pine-studded ridge, facing northeast to where their brothers and sisters (and a couple of cousins) praised the brilliant winter night. I ached with pleasure; I howled again—out of pure joy, not caring if there was a reply.

After several minutes of stillness I picked up my skis. It would be disruptive now to make a lap, grating on the ears to hear the crunch and swish of these artifacts. If I had had the power I'd have floated back up to the cabin, weaving through the birches a foot off the snow, absolutely noiseless, like an apparition of some long-dead Ojibwe shaman. It would have preserved the wolf song for as long as possible, letting the pristine vibrations penetrate unhindered far into the night, deep into my brain. In a way, I was possessed. Contrary to fundamentalist caution, I'd opened my mind as well as my mouth, allowing a wild notion to enter: that it meant something to howl at the moon, that I could intone the vernacular of wild predators.

Surely it's much safer to be enchanted by the bustle of wind-rushed snowflakes. They're beautiful, but dead, and demand nothing. But now I'd talked to timberwolves; for a while I was their "cousin." Like all the living, they demand life, they require respect as well as meat and air. Our human power is vast, and we've obliterated wolves from most of their ancestral range. They were considered enemies, or, at best, nuisances. We offered disrespect. For many humans that's now an old-fashioned attitude. I've long believed in the right of wolves to hunt and live in the forests they inhabited before any men—red or white—arrived on this continent.

But that belief was academic, rooted in ecological studies and the interdependent logic of the biosphere. Under the Wolf Moon, however, the *idea* of *Canis lupus*, of the basic existence of "wolfness," seeped far into my consciousness. I cannot say—even poetically—that I *was* a wolf, or would want to be. But after howling at the moon and hearing a reply, I'll never again feel exclusively human. That's a heavy responsibility. If there were no hunters, there would be no hunted.

For most of the country, wolf song is no longer a common sound. Around Secret Lake it's a little more frequent than New Year's Day, though the wolf population is slowly reviving. Rarity, of course, is part of its potency, but I would gladly hear it more often. It'll be a great day for wolfkind and mankind when I grow complacent and familiar with their music. It's bittersweet that you can live thirty-some years on this planet and howl for the first time.

2

I N   T H E   W I D O W S '   D E N

It's easy, of course, to be enamored of wolves, and it seems only natural to be fascinated by their song. They're big, furry animals akin to our beloved dogs, and they support a rich body of literature seasoned with romance and myth. I heard wolves in the pages of Jack London and Robert Service long before I actually roamed these woods.

It's not so easy to love spiders. My affection is an acquired taste.

I once saw a spider on my left ski tip. I noticed it as I was tucking in to glide down a hill. It was a medium-sized black spider, with two pairs of legs hugging the tip and two pairs resting on the flat of the ski.

It was a mild day by mid-February standards—almost above freezing. Nevertheless, it was still fully winter and I couldn't recall ever seeing a spider outdoors in that season, much less hitching a ride on my cross-country skis.

I leaned into a curve and had to look up for a few moments, concentrating on the track. When I refocused on the tip the spider was gone, lost in a vast crystalline desert—or so it may have seemed from insect perspective. I assumed the spider was in for a rough time. Prey is relatively scarce in February, and recent mornings had been at zero or below. Spiders don't look as though they're terribly resistant to windchill.

I was sorry. I respect spiders, and it's forbidden to kill one in our house. Being eaters of flies and mosquitoes, they're allies. Of course, it's simpler to be benevolent in this part of the world, where I don't expect a black widow or brown recluse to be lurking in ambush beneath the basement stairs. However, I did once pass a stern trial of my loyalty to the arachnid class.

It happened on an East Texas construction crew. I'd been in the region for only a few weeks and was largely ignorant of the local fauna and their lifestyles. For instance, I'd never seen a scorpion before and was blissfully unaware that it was possible to discover one perched on your shoulder while you were relaxing in your bedroom—but that was later.

Our crew was installing a storm drain system for a new office building. One morning my foreman and I were assigned to inspect the older pipeline that we were going to tie into. We found the first manhole, popped off the cast iron lid with a pry bar, and peered into the gloom.

"Manhole" is an oxymoron; these shafts are usually uncongenial environs for humans. Even at their best, manholes are no place for the squeamish or the claustrophobic, and most of us are a little bit of both. This particular hole was an old one—made of brick and about twelve feet deep. A rusty ladder was set into the wall, and a pale green, funguslike sheen coated the bricks.

We stuck our heads below the rim of the circular opening to get the sunlight out of our eyes, and the breath of the hole engulfed our faces. It was dank and musty, tinged with the odor of putrefaction. It smelled sinister,

like a gate into Hades, or the wet throat of a giant sub-
terranean reptile.

As our eyes adjusted to darkness we could see that the
wall wasn't cracked, and the ladder, though slowly rot-
ting, was basically sound. But there appeared to be an
obstruction in the open pipe at the bottom, and someone
would have to climb down to check it out. Years later I
found myself working at a sewage plant, where manholes were many and horrible. We often flipped a coin to
determine who was going to descend into the worst one.
But my foreman in Texas had no use for the democracy of
chance. He simply grunted and hooked a thumb into the
maw. It was my turn; it would always be my turn.

I eased my boots to the top rung of the ladder and
kicked it. Some surface metal flaked off, but most of the
steel was still there. I trusted it with my weight and gingerly felt for the next rung. In a few moments I was fully
below ground. Just as my head sank beneath the rim, the
foreman tapped my hard hat and said, "Wait a minute."
He reached into his toolbox and handed me a ball-peen
hammer.

"What's this for?" I asked.

He grinned. "That's so you can kill all the black widows on the way down."

I laughed. I thought he was joking, trying to spook a
rookie who'd never been in an East Texas manhole. But
he made me take the hammer, so I gripped the ladder and
looked around.

They were everywhere. The top three or four feet of
the hole were cantilevered—each course of brick over-

lapping the one below so that the hole gradually narrowed to the lid. There were numerous angles and upside-down "shelves"—a perfect milieu for spider webs. I spotted three black widows immediately. Given the confines of the hole, they were inches from my face.

My first impulse was to burst into a hammering frenzy—while screaming—but then an irrational thought checked my swing. What if I splattered one and then all the rest (how many hadn't I seen yet?) attacked in a raging swarm of self-defense? It was a fantasy straight out of horror movies and nightmares, but for a moment it seemed plausible down there in the widows' den. After all, I was surrounded.

My second impulse was to fly out of the hole and never return. But the foreman was still grinning, and I suddenly realized that this was a test. Was I worthy of this crew? What was this greenhorn made of? I understood that if I leapt out of that hole the foreman would laugh until he choked, and the story would dog me for the rest of my tenure. No doubt it would generate an unflattering nickname of some sort, and eventually I might be forced into some foolish act of bravado to get it repealed. No, I couldn't jump out of the hole.

I clung to the ladder, paralyzed, and recalled an old curse. As kids, my buddies and I had several noxious habits. One was to collect hundreds of red ants—by ripping apart their hills—and then dump them on top of a black anthill. The ensuing mayhem and death would entertain us for hours—such furious battle! Another cruel game was to catch daddy longlegs and pinch their legs off one by one to see how it affected their stride. We'd been conditioned to treat insects, especially spiders, as enemies.

But one of our gang thought the torture and slaughter were criminal. It was amazing to the rest because he was the neighborhood tough, the kid who would fight at the drop of a hat, and always win. We'd seen Gordy take on older boys nearly twice his size and make up the deficit with simple ferocity. Busted lips and bloody noses— whether the other guy's or his own—didn't faze him.

But killing ants and spiders did. We chided him one day—gently, of course; nobody wanted a squashed nose —about his concern for bugs, and he fumed. The ants and spiders didn't have a chance, Gordy said, and it was a sin to kill them for no reason. Most of us were Catholics, and he conjured up the visions of hell and purgatory that Monsignor and the nuns had so effectively planted in our minds. That's where we were going, he yelled, because we were murderers. I didn't realize until much later that although he could be a vicious brawler, Gordy always had a good reason (at least in his mind) to fight. Our bullying of harmless, helpless insects made no sense to him.

"You dinks'll be sorry!" he shouted. "You'll pay for killing those bugs!" And then instead of hitting someone, Gordy stalked off in disgust. We kept on amputating spider legs. It made us feel macho to do something he wouldn't.

Now I was in a hellhole crawling with black widows. The prophecy had come to pass. A mass murderer of ants and spiders was confronting justice. It wasn't exactly the version of hell that Gordy had in mind, but I was certain that if he could have seen me in that manhole, a right-eous "I told you so" smirk would have lit up his face.

My knuckles went white as I gripped the hammer, but I didn't swing. It was time to repent of old crimes. I scrambled down the ladder to the pipe and started break-ing up a dam of twigs and leaves that had accumulated over the years. The spiders were concentrated near the top of the hole. I didn't find any at the bottom, but for the five minutes I was down there my spine tingled. I was waiting for one of the black widows to drop onto my neck and exact revenge. As I finished the job, I felt one hit my forearm. I started and slapped in a panic, but there was nothing on my skin; it was the power of sugges-tion—and guilt.

I shoved the hammer into my belt and ascended the ladder, my fear abating a little with each upward step. Apparently I was going to escape. Near the top I paused and studied the spiders. This was for the benefit of the foreman; I didn't want to seem in a hurry. But then, un-expectedly, I noticed how beautiful they were—shiny jet black, with gracefully bent legs and the bright orange hourglass pattern on their bodies. I wished I had my cam-era. The backdrop of the intricate webbing, highlighted by a shaft of sunlight from above, was striking. I counted six spiders.

Then one of them darted across the bricks, as quick as a tiger, and my spine was recharged. I climbed out of the hole into fresh air.

"Yeah," I drawled, "I guess there were a few widows down there," as if to say it was all routine to me. The foreman laughed, and we flopped the lid back over the hole.

It's reported that if a Teton warrior encountered a certain kind of spider while on a journey, he would always kill it; otherwise he was sure to have evil luck. But he was careful to hide his identity from the spider because he believed that its soul would urge living spiders to avenge its death. So while crushing the insect the warrior would say, "O Grandfather Spider, the Thunder-beings kill you." The soul of the spider would tell this to its kin, but no harm would be done, because what could spiders do to the Thunder-beings?

The lesson is clear: It is wise to treat spiders with respect. But since I cannot rely upon the ruse of the Thunder-beings, I trust in kindness instead.

It's twenty years since my redemption in the widows' den, and I haven't killed a spider.

3

CONFESSIONS OF A PREDATOR

Although spiders may feel secure in my presence, I have killed other creatures. I'm a predator, and by extension so is anyone who eats meat. But unlike many who consume far more flesh than I—shrink-wrapped and dated—I often face the death of the animals I eat. One late autumn afternoon a couple of years ago was typical.

The Reverend was scrambling in the underbrush, inflamed and snorting. He'd just flushed our quarry. I heard the grouse blast out of the duff—a furious hammering of wings like a burst of machine-gun fire.

I flinched, then froze, the .410 cocked. The flurry of wing beats abruptly ceased. The grouse had apparently stopped in a nearby tree. I was surprised. It was early November, and that late in the season the birds are usually skittish and wary, flying far off through the forest at the least hint of danger. Most of the careless ones are long dead. Possibly this bird was *too* clever. It knew that the canine creature, a natural enemy, couldn't climb trees, so why expend a lot of valuable energy? It seemed that I— the real threat—was undetected.

Stealth was the key. I was thirty feet from where Rev was snuffling at the base of a small fir, but I could barely see him through the tangle. The bird was invisible. Fortunately, the carpet of aspen leaves and fallen needles was damp from a morning snow shower, so I could tread without crunching. I ducked beneath a sweep of balsam boughs and slunk through a clump of aspen saplings. I snapped off a dead twig with my left shoulder, and to me it sounded as sharp as a .22 shot. I paused, shotgun ready, but the grouse didn't fly. With three more cautious steps I had a clear view of The Rev. He whined in excitement. He knew he had the right tree, and he'd start barking any second.

I scanned the branches of the small fir, but sunlight dazzled my eyes; all I could see was shadows and spots. I eased to the left and placed the trunk of a large balsam between me and the sun. It was like spinning a lens into focus. The dazzle dropped away and the fir leapt into sharp silhouette. The profile of the grouse was etched against the sky, stark and black.

I was twenty feet away and exposed to the bird. I expected it to rocket out of the tree and bank away toward deep cover, but it didn't budge. I could hear it softly cooing and clucking.

For a tense two seconds I drew a bead on its head, zeroing in via the tunnel vision that briefly dissolves all other perceptions. Sighting down the barrel of a gun at a live target is a form of meditation, an effective means of channeling the mind. There is an urgency to killing that must be curbed by aiming, and bead and barrel serve as mantra: be steady, be centered.

I fired and the grouse tumbled, flapping to the ground. Its wings pounded at the earth, kicking up brown leaves. As I ran forward the dog lunged over to the body, making little thrusts through the beating, trying to grab the torso.

I nudged him aside (he's not trained as a retriever) and picked up the bird. Its neck was broken, limp and bloody; its eyes were shut tight. Unconsciousness had come quickly, but the grouse still pulsated with energy. I grasped it hard in both hands, pressing the wings to the breast. But who can contain such desperate potency? The strangled spasms of the wings were shunted inward and the little chest heaved with surprising power—four great jolts that spread apart my thumbs before tapering off to final tremors. I relaxed the grip, my fingers wet with blood.

The Rev sat at attention a few feet away with ears perked, nostrils flared, eyes bright as embers. He was still eager, still fired up; he had no choice. There was no ambivalence in his pure hunter's heart. He loves the aroma of blood and would have gladly cleansed my hands if I had let him.

But he cannot lick my soul. I was sorry I'd killed a grouse—again. For a few moments I was paralyzed with regret, staring at the beautiful downy plumage on the breast of the bird. The delicate tones of gray and brown merge in an elaborate mosaic, and you can lose yourself in a labyrinth of subtle shadings and flowing patterns. Each feather is a bold composition, but overlapped and aligned they meld into sophisticated camouflage. I'd shot another masterpiece. I'd riddled living art with lead.

I always caress a grouse for a while, feeling the warmth, admiring the beauty. I always whisper an apology. It's a ritual. If someone should ever see me kneeling reverently in the brush clutching a dead bird, no doubt he or she would cautiously back away.

But I'm not a sportsman. Killing for "sport" is not my style. I'm a predator, and I kill for meat. When we enjoyed a steady, adequate income, the shotgun laid dormant for a decade. I had no excuse for killing grouse.

I know of some hunters who will only shoot at a grouse on the wing, who think it "unsporting" to blast one off a perch or on the ground. They'll go so far as to shake a tree to force a reluctant bird to take off. It's supposed to be more fun. But if the main objective is good shooting, then why not stick with skeet or trap? Why not shatter clay pigeons instead of ripping flesh and blood? Why kill for amusement?

"But we keep the meat," say the sportsmen. Sure, most of the grouse end up in the freezer. Some of them are even consumed. But I've seen it happen often: birds rest next to the ground beef and ice cream for several months or a year—long enough to expiate guilt—and then they're thrown out. You can't eat desiccated freezer-burned grouse can you? A "good" sportsman always takes the meat home, but he's not required to use it.

After a few moments of silence, I pulled my knife and dressed out the bird. The Rev tap-danced in place as the dismemberment began, wired a shade to the left of wild. I dug into the hot carcass for a handful of entrails and tossed them at his feet. He gulped them down then licked the leaves where they'd landed. Such a snack keeps his nose focused on our purpose.

And who am I kidding? I enjoy it as much as he does. Yes, we eat every bird, and yes, they do supplement our supermarket supplies, but I don't do it exclusively for the meat. I'm a predator, but I'm also a hypocrite. We won't starve if I don't kill grouse. I delight in the hunt—I'm playing God, wielding the intoxicating power of life and death. I find zest in the entrails. There's something profoundly elemental about the act of evisceration. Only with my knife can I delve this deeply toward the core of a great mystery.

Many times I've pinched the heart of a grouse in my fingers, amazed that such a small glob of guts is the engine of a flying machine. I've poked through the nest of organs cupped in the palm of my hand, fascinated. Only moments before, this slimy pile was an intricate living system, an energized biological creation that mocks the capabilities of our most advanced automatons. How can it be? How can blood and mush be organized to form a living being of such splendor and function? Even when I eat this grouse and its flesh merges with mine, I will not know. It's a maddening paradox. Each time I make this deathly probe, I'm humbled by the wonder of life.

And so I don't kill grouse for base and frivolous sport. I kill for a sense of awe. It scares the hell out of me, and someday I'm going to stop.

4

WHEN EAGLES SCREAM

I'm not the only killer around. In fact, I used to know a guy who was called "Killer." It was a joke, like calling a bald man Curly or a white dog Blackie. His demeanor was that of a quiet village priest, as gentle as a New Age prophet. He tended his tomato plants as if they had souls, as if God had personally charged him with the solemn responsibility. But it was a double irony, because "Killer" had really killed. It was a few years back, in a place he called "Vietgone."

"It was over the rim of the world," he said. "Over the rainbow, but not a dreamland. Not at all."

His real name was Malcolm ("a motherly corruption of Malcontent"), and he didn't look the part of a warrior. Even with props—perhaps a beret and bandoleer—he wouldn't have looked like a guy who had earned a Silver Star, a Distinguished Service Cross, a Vietnamese Croix de Guerre, and two Purple Hearts. Not that war heroes look like anything in particular, but he didn't fit the Hollywood stereotype.

I wouldn't know about the medals at all, if it hadn't been for a pint of Yukon Jack and a northern Minnesota January night. We were holed up in his cabin on the banks of the Little Fork River, stalemated at chess and focused on the glass doors of his wood stove. It was thirty degrees below zero at the rooftop, and the stove's vigorous draft was cheerily sucking Arctic air in through every leaky notch of the weathered pine logs. The whiskey offered a false sense of warmth and security. It was also quiet, as still as hard winter stars. Even the river was muted. Before dark we'd skied down to the bank and tried to hear the rapids. In the spring it's a roaring cascade, a class II whitewater run that surges to the roots of the basswoods. But now it was low, sneaking under the ice. We could discern a faint murmuring, a whisper of current saying almost nothing as it slipped away to Ontario.

But Mal (I don't call him "Killer"; that's a tavern moniker used by casual acquaintances) said a great deal. He'd had enough of the reserve of pawns and rooks, and a shared fire is shared counsel. We passed the bottle, relishing the vapors as if they were the smoke of a peace pipe.

The medals were in a slim wooden case; I'd noticed it on the windowsill as we played chess. The cover was embossed with the head of a bald eagle, its hooked beak agape, the eyes alert and deadly—the logo of the 101st Airborne.

We were halfway through the whiskey when Mal suddenly rose and fetched the case. He sat down and stared at it a moment, brushing lightly at the lid as if he were holding an ancient artifact he'd just unearthed.

"I dug it out this morning," he said. "Looked at it over a cup of coffee—like it was normal or something."

I was fascinated, filled with the morbid curiosity of a male who'd never Been There. I was ready to hear screaming eagles.

But Mal started talking about lawyers; he'd been one for a while. The GI bill had helped him through law school, and he'd gone to work for a firm in Duluth. It was five names long, an odd arrangement of ethnic syllables that sounded, said Mal, "like a trunk tumbling down a flight of stairs." He'd entertained visions of Advocacy, of slugging it out for Justice. For him the law was a nexus with a higher form of life, emblematic of civilization. But it was also a stylized form of combat, a direct confrontation of adversaries under the auspices of and sanctioned by the state, that is, of the people. It was necessary, prudential; but often bitter, and sometimes dirty.

"I surprised myself," said Mal. "I found I wasn't ready for lawyering. I was getting some of the same feelings in court I used to have in Vietgone. Made me nervous."

He said he'd probably return to the law one day— maybe try to get on the legal staff of some outfit like Friends of the Earth or Defenders of Wildlife—do something positive and durable for the biosphere. We'd been this route before. I kidded, reminding him that in the past two years he'd planted 3,000 trees on his forty acres, and it would be hard to top that for pure environmental action.

"Yeah, action." he replied. "I guess I'm sort of addicted to action. Attorneys don't sweat enough."

Mal left Duluth and bought his forty acres of brush. It's remote, rough-hewn land, and he loved it. In true Koochiching County fashion, he worked at part-time jobs: logging, chiefly in black spruce bogs in winter; an occasional painting or roofing job; and seasonal forest fire fighting for the Department of Natural Resources. That's where I met him—at a brush fire off County Highway 5. There were two helicopters making bucket drops on hot spots, and Mal was in his glory, once again bathed with rotor wash in the heat of "battle." He said he'd always liked choppers, and fire duty was a way to enjoy air operations that had nothing to do with killing people.

But in January it was the chain saw, cutting spruce and being paid by the stick—twenty-two cents apiece. If he worked very hard, he could make three hundred dollars a week, assuming there was a logger who needed help.

Mal liked working in the woods. He was born and raised in Kansas, and he was endlessly intrigued by the compressed distances of the forest. He grew up with far horizons, with wide, hot skies and open land. In the woods he felt comfortably hidden, sheltered like a camouflaged fawn. With the zeal of a newcomer, he'd studied forest ecology. He became an amateur silviculturist, and suspected he had missed his calling. He also delved into the folklore of ancient forest cultures, and that's where the case of medals came in.

At least that's what he told me when I finally asked. He was still talking about the law when I bluntly interrupted.

"Forget lawyers. What's in the box?"

Well, we had to build up to that. He had to present his case, mold the jury into the shape of his opinion.

The day before, he'd been out cutting. But the boss had pulled him out of a spruce bog and set him to felling in a stand of mature aspen. The best saw bolts were destined to be made into chopsticks at the new factory in Hibbing and shipped to the Orient. "Can't seem to get away from Asia," he grinned. "Of course, it's a big place."

After he'd downed several trees, he stopped to fashion a "story pole." The aspens had to be bucked up into one-hundred-inch "sticks," and rather than tediously measure each one with a tape (or inaccurately eyeball them), a sawyer will cut a straight aspen sapling to exactly one hundred inches, and thus have a light and convenient measuring rod, or story pole.

Mal said that as he trimmed his pole he had a sense of academic déjà vu. There was something strangely familiar about the aspen rod. And as he marked off the trunks into sticks, he recalled a tidbit of anthropological arcana. Ancient Celtic peoples of the British Isles had been tree worshippers, developing a complex body of lore about the various species. The aspen, probably because of its rapid regeneration and growth, had been regarded as a symbol of rebirth. So in subsequent centuries, aspen rods had been used to measure the length of corpses and coffins.

As he bucked up the trees he'd just killed, Mal meditated on that. "You know how the mind jumps," he said. "Suddenly I wasn't a simple logger anymore. I was a murderous undertaker, methodically measuring my victims for efficient transport to the great aspen underworld. From there, of course, it was only a short hop to Vietgone."

The imagery of the carefully gauged coffin triggered a surge of memories that welled to the surface like pressurized, incandescent magma. Mal took another pull on the Yukon Jack and told me about it.

After boot camp and jump school at Fort Campbell, Kentucky, he'd gone home on extended leave. Mike, his best friend from high school, had a II-S deferment and was a freshman at Wichita State. Mal had gone there to visit, staying in the dorm and bootlegging food with a borrowed meal ticket. He was gung ho, on fire with the military enthusiasm instilled by the demanding regimen of an elite unit headed for combat. Over the course of a very liquid, college-boy-macho-party weekend, he talked Mike into not only joining the army, but also becoming a paratrooper—"the only part of the army worth a damn." They chanted together, sloshing in beer: "Airborne! Airborne! Have you heard? We're gonna jump from the big-ass birds!"

Mike dropped out of college and made it to jump school. Upon graduation he was assigned to the 173d Airborne, and a few months after Mal he was duly shipped to Southeast Asia. Unlike Mal, he was killed—mangled by a mortar round.

Mal escorted the remains to Kansas and was in charge of the military funeral. The coffin was closed. Mike's mother wanted to look inside, but Mal wouldn't allow it. He conducted the ceremony with rigid precision, handling the pallbearers as he had his machine-gun squad, with an eye toward survival. He bore up under the strain like the professional he was—nearly to the end. He and a sergeant from the 173d folded up the flag that was draped over the casket. Their white gloves marched from crease to crease, measuring—quick, sure, practiced—buffers between bare flesh and sacred icon. Mal strode over to Mike's mother. As he handed her the flag, he choked. He'd spent almost as much time in that woman's house as he had in his own. She'd fed him, made him wash his hands, hugged him, even spanked him. In return, Mal had convinced her son to become a paratrooper. He saluted. Then he strode over to his own mother, buried his head in her shoulder, and sobbed.

The memories burned, and Mal had to take a break from sawing trees. He replaced his aspen story pole with a chunk of nearby balsam, opting to break with ancient tradition. That night he dreamed about it all: dropping into a hot LZ not with his M-60 machine gun but with a sharpened aspen stake. He and his unit were chewed up, and the NVA came around to measure their corpses with chopsticks. It was a long night.

In the morning he brought out the case of medals.

"There was a time," he said, "when I was going to do something stupid, like throw these things away; or hawk them. But I realized that was vain. It was even a little sick, like a self-imposed lobotomy. It wouldn't do anyone any good, least of all me. Or Mike."

Then he told me about the afternoon he'd collected some of those tokens of glory.

"It happened in the woods," he said, "on some Vietnamese forty that we tore the hell out of with bullets and shells." He was directing an M-60 machine-gun squad during an intense, close-quarters firefight. Two of his people were killed in the first several minutes of action. At one point he was firing the M-60 from behind a downed tree, when a bullet struck the log. He actually saw it. The wood splintered, and his vision was kicked into "a weird slow-motion kind of seeing." He watched the bullet approach his face and slam into the bridge of his nose—lodged directly between his eyes. It knocked him flat on his back.

His initial reaction was rage. He leapt to his feet, stripped off his web gear, and yelled, "Fuck this shit!" Then, stalking upright through the woods where he'd low-crawled all day, he worked his way back to an LZ where the wounded were being prepped for medevac.

He didn't realize he was drenched in blood down to his boots, and one of the medics fixed him with a white-faced stare that convinced Mal he was going to die. He stretched out on a poncho, suddenly exhausted. A medic was hovering over him a few minutes later when he decided he'd better return to his M-60. He had to be forced back down. He couldn't recall the medevac.

These days he has severe headaches occasionally, and he wears thick eyeglasses. He's also bothered by pain in his left leg from time to time—a holdover from a shrapnel wound. The army awarded him a 10 percent disability.

Aside from pain and the meager benefits, the medals were the only substantial, hands-on legacy of four years of his life. Four very important years. Historic years. And they're beautiful. He passed me the case and I handled the talismans. The Purple Heart, with its pearly cameo bust of George Washington, is a fine piece of jewelry.

Small payment, to be sure, for a bullet in the face, but pretty nonetheless.

"Look at them," said Mal. "They're a part of what I am." And then, slightly embarrassed, but emboldened by Yukon Jack, he asked, "Do you think I'm a little bit evil?"

I laughed. I shook my head and gave him a friendly shove with my free hand. "Aren't we all, Mal?"

The cliché is, of course, absolutely correct. Time heals; if not all, then at least most. And I was gratified to be sharing a bottle and a fire with a man who, though he had killed, was certainly not a killer.

5

T I R E S   D o n ' t   f e e d

It's up to us to hone such distinctions—between a killer and a murderer, between the way things are and the way we feel things should be. Nature, that is, everything besides us and what we create, has little use for our quibbling. You can certainly argue that we are a part of Nature, and may even temporarily convince yourself, but in our heart of hearts we really don't believe it. As a species, we humans most often view ourselves as a collective deus ex machina, either foisted on, or bequeathed to the world—depending upon your philosophy or your mood. It's why we so regularly intervene in the lives of fellow creatures. We'd probably resent it if songbirds suddenly decided they should feed us all winter, or if black bears opened a hunting season on hikers and berry pickers. (They'd have my full support if they targeted ATV users, and imposed no bag limit.) But we casually disrupt the lives of animals as a matter of course and tend to brand the human protesters of our heavy-handedness as fanatics or lunatics. We accept it as our mission to both exploit and rescue other life forms. What else are gods for? We can't seem to help it, and I'm not advocating a strict hands-off policy toward animals. I shall continue to pour a quarter-ton of sunflower seed through our birdfeeders annually. The grosbeaks don't *appear* resentful.

But it might be an enlightening exercise if we'd culti-
vate more deference toward the animal kingdom. Henry
Beston captured our most common attitude when he
wrote, "We patronize them for their incompleteness, for
their tragic fate of having taken form so far below ourselves. And therein we err, and greatly err. For the animal
shall not be measured by man." Perhaps our standards of
success and achievement on the planet—in the universe—do not necessarily encompass all life; our agenda,
though prominent, may not be the only one. The Judeo-
Christian ethic, arguably the strongest strain in Western
philosophy, outlines our interspecies strategy in the
book of Genesis: "Be fruitful, multiply, fill the earth and
subdue it, mastering the fish in the sea, the birds of the
air, and every living creature that crawls on the earth."
Well, it's been done—to a fault. Now what? I suggest
courtesy and respect (and human birth control).

But it's hard to be considerate when you believe you
rule the planet, and not long ago I was reminded of my
place.

I admit stopping wasn't my idea. I noticed the turtle as
we drove by, but the image didn't really register. It was in
the other lane, about a foot from the centerline and
tucked inside its shell. County Highway 5 was busy, and
a ponderous turtle traverse was almost surely destined
for disaster. Besides, the turtle rested just below the crest
of a hill, and even a conscientious motorist might not see
the traveler before it was too late to swerve or brake.

But none of that penetrated my driving-dazed consciousness until my wife, Pam, said, "Let's stop and help
it."

"What?"

"That turtle back there. It needs to get across the high-way."

"Oh."

I pulled over and made a U-ball at the base of the hill. Certainly we should help, and I was irritated I hadn't thought of it. County 5 isn't a toll road—isn't even within a hundred miles of one—but I figure aiding turtle crossings is part of the fee (or penance) owed by humans for the privilege of plying our asphalt rivers. Lord knows that the number of deer, rabbits, grouse, porcupines, and other animals we've smashed with our vehicles is astronomical. If ravens and vultures are by chance reasoning creatures, I suspect they consider highways gifts from their gods and the lifeblood of the cosmos.

I hurried back to the turtle, parked as far over on the shoulder as I could, and switched on the emergency flashers. I'll never forget how an acquaintance once zigzagged to avoid killing a rabbit and lost control of his car. He fishtailed and hit the ditch, demolishing his Renault and inflicting a permanent back injury on himself. These highway missions must be kept in perspective. That rabbit's health didn't appear quite as important from the vantage of a hospital bed.

I scampered out into the roadway and gingerly grasped the carapace in both hands, holding it away from my body (I've had them pee on me—or at least that's what I speculate the fluid was). The turtle poked its head and feet out for an instant, then withdrew. I imagined a cartoonist's thought bubble rising from the head opening:

"Now what?" We were at the centerline, and my neck tingled, feeling the creature's vulnerability. From tail to snout the turtle was less than eight inches long. To negotiate the highway from ditch to ditch would be the equivalent of my crawling across an exposure as wide as a football field, in the path of hurtling machines as big as four-story buildings. Small wonder she hid in her shell. I assumed this was a female; it was late May, and the hazardous trek was probably an egg-laying venture.

I gently placed her at the edge of the far shoulder, facing the safety of the tall grass. She didn't budge, but after we drove over the hill, turned around at the bottom, and returned, she was gone. Pam and I exchanged a smile. It was a small kindness, costing little, but it generated warmth.

One night, a week later, we turned into our gravel driveway and I dodged a turtle that was digging in the sand. A nest. It's happened near that spot in our road every spring we've lived here.

"We can mark it in the morning," Pam said. We always ribbon off the buried eggs until they hatch or they're eaten by predators, forcing ourselves and visitors to swing wide for a few weeks.

But unfortunately it was Memorial Day weekend, and our rural lakeside community was infected with the bacillus of "tourists" from town. How else to put it? They've a right to be here, of course, but every summer weekend—especially Memorial Day, the Fourth, Labor Day—the roadsides are sprinkled with garbage, noise levels increase tenfold, traffic (normally an alien concept) becomes a concern, and inevitably there's an accident, fire, or other incident requiring emergency response. I savor rain on the holidays.

A particular irritation is that our "driveway"—almost a quarter-mile long—becomes a "cruisin' " route. Vehicles approach the homestead at all hours, inflaming The Reverend (his job, after all), and thus waking us. We're spoiled. Our nights are mostly serene, embellished by loon song, cricket song, wolf song, and rustling leaves. I'm not sure why tourists insist on exploring our road. It's clearly marked as a private drive, and therefore an occupied dead end. They're invariably teenagers—I can judge the quality of their sound systems from our bedroom— and my theory is they're searching for secluded spots to park, driving "upstream" on narrow channels in order to breed like spawning trout. With minds dulled by alcohol and preoccupied with potential copulation, our discreet signs are invisible to them.

At half past midnight, The Rev plunged into a barking frenzy, and I heard a vehicle rumbling up the driveway. Even though roused from sleep, Pam whispered, "I hope they don't run over the turtle."

I stumbled to the window and watched headlights emerge from the woods. Some nondescript rock 'n' roll meshed with engine and power train clatter, accented by peals of adolescent laughter. As they reached the yard I heard snatches of talk—"log house . . . turn back." But the driver wasn't satisfied to merely depart. He spun around and floored it, gouging ruts in the grass and splattering the fence with divots. Punk! I entertained a fantasy about my .410 and number six bird shot.

At around two A.M. a second car drove in, but I didn't get up. I heard Pam mumble, " . . . damn . . . tourists . . . turtle . . . "

In the morning I had an errand at the store, so I drove out slowly, creeping around the corner before the traditional nesting ground. I passed more ruts, and a discarded beer can.

The turtle was there, in precisely the spot we'd seen her the night before. Her shell was crushed, but she was still attempting to dig.

I make part of my living as a wildland firefighter, and over the years I've seen dead animals on the fire ground (though not as many as you might think). Until that morning, the most pathetic sight I'd encountered was a blackened wetland area (during the '88 drought) where a particularly hot blaze had overtaken dozens of turtles. Some were burned completely out of their shells, leaving blackened husks, while others retained a charred foot or tail. I envisioned a "running dream," in which you're sprinting from some monster as fast as you're able, but you can't get away. The turtles were probably clawing at the grass even as they burned. I brought home one of the empty shells as a reminder of the hazards of the fire ground.

But this turtle in our driveway was more horrible. Her shell was cracked into jagged fifths, partially cemented with clotted blood and swollen tissue. Wads and tangles of yellowish intestine bulged from the gaps at her left side, and the sand beneath was gooey and stained. But her head was out and all four feet were scratching—albeit weakly—at the dirt. Through the broken shell I could see cartilage and muscles twitching in concert with feet. She didn't realize she was dead.

For a moment I helplessly raged at the idiots who'd run her over, hurling curses into innocent air. Her butchers were the same riffraff who left ruts and a beer can in our driveway. Even so, I realized that in all likelihood they hadn't recognized her. In the glare of headlights she'd looked like a rock, a slab of bark, or even a pothole. Perhaps they noticed nothing at all. She probably hadn't been crushed on purpose.

That was even more sickening. Premeditated destruction at least implies thought and attention. Purpose can be countered with purpose. Far more insidious is the apathy or ignorance that doesn't even sense disaster. As a species we humans are arrogant, assuming, as Beston wrote, that all other creatures are lesser than we. Maybe they are (since we make the judgments). But our attitude of blithe supremacy makes us reckless and clumsy, unmindful of our neighbors (who may be sleeping, or laying eggs) and our neighborhood. I believe the water, atmosphere, and soil will continue under threat of despoilation as long as we're heedless of mother turtles in the roadway.

I'm not blameless in these matters either, but I briefly hated the driver who'd mangled this turtle. At least I'd seen her—even in headlights. And now, through no fault of mine, I had to deal with the terrible shreds of her life. If she'd been squealing or moaning it would've been easier to finish the killing. Even though she struggled, there was no sound of injury. She was utterly silent; it was unnerving. For a crazy minute I studied the damage and wondered if she might still lay her eggs and live—or at least lay the eggs, so the cycle of life could be recast. But no, no; such hope was only a defense mechanism for myself. I didn't want to kill her. But it seemed the decent thing to do.

Although repugnant, I decided the surest method was to complete the crushing. I returned to my car, backed up, and, aiming with the fender, carefully hit her square on with the left front wheel. There was a bump, and then a giving-way flattening sensation transmitted through the tire, suspension, and seat—a deus ex machina indeed, an amphibian Götterdämmerung. Stalked and finished. And tires don't even feed.

I picked up the carcass and carried it into the woods. Pam would have to know, but she wouldn't have to see.

I mused that one cause of this tragedy was weather. An early thaw in April advanced the season, and my phenology records showed that the usual events of early June— wild roses blooming, first firefly, turtles laying—were happening in late May. In a "normal" year, the mother turtle would have missed Memorial Day weekend on our road, and thus might have been saved. No comfort, of course, but a way to share the blame.

I continued on to the store to buy a Sunday newspaper—a glutton for punishment, I guess.

6

AN APOCALYPSE OF
MAYFLIES

But gloom is too easy, and clouds the vision. The Sunday paper, for all its ill wind, also includes Shoe and the brash weirdos of "The Far Side." Properly crumpled it makes an excellent lighter for cedar kindling, quickly inducing a stout draft in the chimney. It's also recyclable.

So are all life forms. Death cycles back into the food chain, both directly and indirectly, and is eventually indistinguishable from birth. Carcasses are nourishment—for soil, plants, other creatures—and as soon as my mother turtle was dead she initiated a new career.

Endings and beginnings fit a wave pattern—crest and trough, trough and crest, in sinuous movement through space and time. For me, it's easier to see this when I'm in a canoe on some remote lake or river, and my only job is to notice events. Most are relatively small and quiet. In conventional human habitat, many small but important events are readily missed.

A couple of years ago, Pam and I and some friends were paddling a portion of the Kawishiwi River in the Boundary Waters Canoe Area Wilderness. The river was pregnant. In the main channel, we paddled past three active gull nests in a few hundred yards. Nervous mothers eyed us from atop single-rock islands where they'd tacked their grass incubators. Later, while foraging for kindling near a deadfall on the bank, I was startled by a sudden lunging at my feet. I jumped—partly because we'd just met three garter snakes sunning themselves on the ledge rock, and a viper attack (though unlikely from a harmless garter) was my first thought. Actually, my assailant was a female ruffed grouse, and as I quickly backed away, I counted seven eggs in the nest I'd nearly stepped on. Since morning we'd tallied two dozen ducklings—tiny mallards and mergansers bobbing along in the wakes of solicitous hens. Birds, at least, were thriving in the annual greenhouse effect of mid-June, and the Kawishiwi and its banks were charged with life.

Despite the alien sheen of our fiberglass and aluminum canoes, it was possible to sustain the illusion of being simply other forest residents—players as well as observers. We were migrating, slipping further into the wilderness toward the ceremonial ground of a campsite and the nightly ritual fires that purge a measure of civilization's anxieties.

But we never quite mesh. Our canoes are quiet, but more like dreadnoughts than driftwood. Our paddles slice and glisten, but they're closer to props than fins. We're part of the wilderness by definition, just because we're there, but are seldom exactly in phase—usually a few wavelengths to the side or behind. We don't soften granite like nesting gulls, or fearlessly attack giants like a mothering grouse. We have our skills and aptitudes, of course, and flourish where others would perish, but I'm often envious of wildlife. There's so much elegance and beauty, such magnificently innate wisdom and power in the creatures we automatically deem beneath our station.

From this vibrant sentience arises a wellspring of drama—happenings as vivid and potent as the stark images of human ferment that we see on the nightly news. It's more than the fierce thunderstorms that churn these border lakes to froth, or the phantasmic northern lights that glow like fire in the water. It's the "little" things, the living things, that evoke the depth of wonder that challenges our perception. The same day we witnessed such drama.

A half hour before sunset, when the breeze had mellowed to whiffs of cedar scent, and the river was as placid as a pond, Pam and I paddled out to fish. She unlimbered her fly rod and made long graceful casts from the bow as I eased along the shore of a fecund-looking backwater.

It was peaceful—still, and suffused with dense yellow light—but there was too much competition in the fishing. The air over the river was speckled with mayflies, seeming to materialize out of the atmosphere itself. They hovered erratically, like snowflakes backlit by sundown, then settled onto the water and twitched, blatantly offering themselves to the fish. The twitching made it seem like a blunder, as if the mayflies had accidentally swirled to the surface and were now trying to rise. But their vibrations were a beacon, concentric ripples spreading away like the stylized symbol of a transmitter antenna. And the panfish and bass below were tuned in, rising suddenly from the dark water to snatch a fly—a plop and gurgle, then a wider set of ripples. The handmade fly at the end of Pam's line was lost in this apocalypse of mayflies.

She was about to switch to her bait-casting rod and try for northern pike, when we noticed some vigorous splashing at the base of a rock ledge. At first we thought it was a big fish, but the thrashing was too wild and prolonged. I pushed the canoe closer.

"It's two snakes!" Pam said.

"Are you sure?" I paddled up to the escarpment.

It was a single snake, about thirty inches long, and its jaws were splayed wide and clasped to the spongy white throat of a large frog. The serpent was writhing furiously, trying to coil around the frog—or so it appeared. But then it slithered its "tail" out of the water and into a crevice in the rock. Gaining purchase, it dragged almost half its length into the cleft, attempting to pull its victim out of the river. The frog twisted and rolled, mouth agape, and threw a leg around the snake, jerking it back into the water. They wrestled and corkscrewed together, first one on top, then the other. The frog flopped a leg onto the wet rock, established a grip, and tried to tug the snake out of the water. The snake yanked it back, and the surging battle continued. Again the black-and-yellow garter managed to shove its tail into the crevice and almost pulled the frog into the rock. But the amphibian pushed off the ledge underwater and heaved the snake with it.

We were five feet from the death struggle, watching like Olympians from above, and I resisted the impulse to intervene. We were rooting for the frog—an unwarranted bias that probably would have been shared by most humans—but this was none of our business, and snakes have a right to feed and survive. Although the digestive capacity of reptiles is legendary, I told Pam I thought the frog was simply too big for this particular snake.

It was either that or the snake tired, for a few moments later it released the frog, stuck its tail end into the cleft, and shot out of sight so smoothly and quickly that we were both startled. It was like a retracting rubber band, a blur, and it raised the hair on my neck.

The frog began to breaststroke away from the ledge in a straight line. It was odd. I'd never seen a frog swim like that for an extended period. A slick dive or darting push to the shelter of lily pads or a half-sunken snag is what I would've expected, but the frog seemed to have forsaken one of the prime characteristics of a wild creature—elusiveness. It was plodding along the surface, mechanically, lifelessly. Was it dazed by the battle? For several yards it followed us as we paddled away. It was Pam's theory that our presence had distracted the snake and caused it to release the frog, and the hapless amphibian now viewed us as saviors. Why not?

But presently the frog veered away, stroking for the middle of the river and leaving a discernible wake.

I studied the watery trail for a few moments, and it hit me: "It's fishing for northerns too," I said.

About five minutes later I heard a splash out in the main channel, and swiveled on my seat. The frog was gone. Only a set of widening ripples remained. A greater mouth than the snake's had risen from the river and gobbled the swimmer in an instant. I imagined a three- or four-pound northern pike, as sleek and swift as a torpedo, with teeth like a barracuda.

"And you think you've had bad days," I quipped. But I was struck by the pattern. The frog resembled the mayflies, persistently transmitting its presence, offering (?) itself to the fish. Had it also offered itself to the snake? Had the snake merely failed, or had we indeed interrupted the process with our gawking? Was the frog compelled to try again? It wasn't flattering to see ourselves as meddlers rather than saviors, but I think it's incomparably beautiful to visualize one creature—perhaps old, diseased, or otherwise short on time—presenting itself as sustenance to another, facilitating and useful to the bitter end. Is there, under certain circumstances, an ecological compact among animals, a mutual acceptance of necessary death? Does a member of one species "choose" to enrich another in order to further the general scheme of things? Is the so-called web of life even more complex and subtle than we dare think?

We humans almost universally view death as tragic. Why? How can something that happens to one and all without fail not be more easily accepted—perhaps even celebrated as one more rite of passage? Our final twitchings are seen as ghastly; the mayflies, I think, are dancing.

It's easy for me to wish and speculate as I sit in our canoe on a tranquil river, aglow in the benevolence of a summer twilight. Only the brain twitches, resonating with the artistry of the world and the lucent lives of the creatures.

At this same season, in June 1852, Thoreau wrote in his journal, "The perception of beauty is a moral test." And the beauty of the life of that wilderness river led me to a moral conclusion: death in the wild is good; not necessarily pleasant and painless, but worthwhile, and perhaps often welcome.

And to what or whom shall I offer my life? When the time comes, will I be as privileged as a frog or a mayfly? Will I dare to present myself?

If we are greater than the animals, it's only because we articulate definitions of greatness. I know that in all likelihood I won't end up as a meal for a northern pike. I cannot know that my death will mean more than that. I hope it'll mean no less. In the meantime I shall paddle the rivers as much as possible. "We are as much as we see," wrote Thoreau. "Faith is sight and knowledge."

7

THE RED AND THE
SCAT

The trouble is, we're not always sure what we see, or why we see it. Pam saw two black bears wearing bright red collars tumble out of a maple tree. She said that I ambled over to talk to them, but they removed their heads and became belligerent. This happened right outside our bedroom window, but I'm a bit fuzzy on the details because, regrettably, I wasn't actually *in* Pam's dream. Such bears would be sensational—even without red collars—but in the realm of backwoods visions they'd by no means be unique. After a decade and a half of living in the forest, it seems merely a technicality that Pam encountered these odd bears in her sleep, and not in waking daylight.

A few years ago, while paddling down the middle reaches of the Big Fork River, a wild stream that winds through remote, relatively pristine territory, I was startled to feel the water tremble. I mean, the river was vibrating; I could sense tremors through the hull of the canoe. I glanced at my companion and met wide, darting eyes; it wasn't my imagination. Then we heard the pounding—a surging rataplan from somewhere on the right bank that was being transmitted from shore to river to canoe. I stood up in the stern to scan the bank.

It was steep, with tall July grass burgeoning to the water's edge, and beyond the waving crest I could see the crowns of aspen and balsam fir—the rampart of a high forest meadow encompassing a sharp bend in the river.

The pounding intensified, and we clutched our paddles in our laps, paralyzed with fascination and raptly staring at the rim of the bank.

Just before the hollow drumming reached a crescendo, the first creature—large, white, and running hard—burst over the edge of the slope, seeming to tear out of the earth into the sky. It was quickly followed by another and another, and then jostling knots of four and six at a time. It took a moment to register, and then we yelped in surprise. Horses! A surging herd of three dozen—a full range of colored flanks galloping along the top of the bank and led by a white steed with a black mane and tail. Only a rush of unicorns could have been more stunning in this northwoods ambience. The horses rumbled along the bank for a hundred yards, splaying the belly-high grass and casting up globs of red clay in a bare spot, then cut back into the meadow and were gone.

It was a cameo appearance of the unexpected, and I laughed aloud, still grasping a dry paddle. The compelling impression was of a staged event, as if the equine show had been carefully timed to coincide with the brief span of our passage on that stretch of river. Are horses bright enough to show off and purposely amaze?

Or had the horses been as nonplussed as we? The contrast between northwoods stream and horse herd was sharp, a conjunction of two worlds—Paul Bunyan and Wyatt Earp, Hiawatha and Geronimo, a bull moose and a stallion, spruce bog and dry plains. Perhaps, I suggested to my companion, we'd intersected a rare space-time nexus, and that speculation about "multiple universes" arising from quantum theory had merit, and the horses were "really" in Wyoming (or "Wyoming Prime," its counterpart in one of the alternate universes), and for a few moments we, or they, or both, were shunted through a Minnesota-Wyoming cosmic synapse (a perceptual overload circuit breaker?) that allowed us to briefly experience each other. Now we were back on the "real" Big Fork, and they'd slipped back into their "real" Wyoming. My partner thought it sounded good.

Nevertheless, it was more likely (in our present conceptual framework) that our encounter with the horses was coincidence, and although such herds are not common in this part of the world, they aren't completely foreign. Someone with land on the river was a horse rancher, I suppose. But the episode would have been far less startling if I'd experienced it in a dream, and the dream-like quality of the image was striking.

My horses seemed "more real" than Pam's bears, but when she described the red-collared beasts I could picture them clearly. When I described the horses, she could easily imagine them. How fine the distinction between what we term reality and what we often brush off as dream. How natural it seems to experience the "unnatural."

Early one morning about five years ago, Pam rose from bed and looked out the bedroom window (the same window in which the red-collared bears would later appear). She gasped, and actually jumped away from the glass. "Who's that!" she cried. There had been a man dressed all in red staring up at her. I rushed to the pane and saw a red jacket disappearing into the brush. In November I would have assumed this was an errant deer hunter, but it was summer, and it's unusual to see anyone in the woods near our relatively remote cabin. Curious, I threw on some clothes and hurried outside.

At the edge of the yard I caught sight of him. He'd stopped and was looking back through the forest at the house. He saw me and quickly turned to duck beneath the boughs of a large fir. Why was he fleeing? (Why was I pursuing?) I followed and steadily gained on him, focused on the bobbing red jacket, knowing the man was heading down a point of land that tapered off to bog on three sides. It was a natural trap, and he'd have no place to go without wading. I was forty yards away when he hit the bog, and I saw him pause. I bent to plunge through some alders, and when I looked up he was gone.

I humped to the edge of the bog, expecting to see him either slogging through the sphagnum moss, or crouched in hiding nearby. Neither. It had taken me less than a minute to reach the point where I'd seen him last, but he'd vanished. My astonishment was like a punch in the chest. I stopped to listen intently. It would have been easy to hear him crunching through the woods on that quiet morning. Nothing. I thoroughly searched the bog edge (even looking up into the trees), and found no spot that would conceal a man dressed in red.

That's what really spooked me—red jacket, red cap, red pants, and in a matter of seconds he'd disappeared. If he'd been all in camouflage I could've rationalized, made excuses for my failure. Yet even then I'd been so close, so absolutely certain I had him. My wonder was tinged with fear. This was weird, and I had no explanation. I wasn't sure what frightened me more—that a person could just strangely vanish, or that someone was that accomplished at stealth. It bothered me for a while, and this is the first time I've told the story. The aura of eeriness has mellowed, but, after all, it was a man (apparently) we saw. Two of our neighbors once saw Sasquatch.

They were separate incidents, but in the same area of woods around the same time. While grouse hunting, one neighbor encountered a large hairy beast on two legs, and was so close and so startled that he actually took a shot at it. The other neighbor, along with two other witnesses, had stopped on a dirt road at night. They left the engine running and headlights on as they went into the ditch to pee. The creature entered the beam of headlights and began to approach on two legs. It was "at least seven or eight feet tall," and the three women pissed on themselves as they sprinted back to the car and roared off.

Both these neighbors have lived in the woods for years (the grouse hunter all his life) and swear the creature was no bear. Neither of them was drunk, stoned, or emotionally stressed. They (and others) believe they saw Sasquatch, or Bigfoot. No one, of course, has evidence to the contrary, and I wouldn't be surprised to hear of someone finally proving the existence of a species of large, elusive primates in the wild areas of North America. Why not? Just the other day I saw something far more shocking.

In the middle of a forest path were several dainty blue butterflies clustered on a dark, livid heap of bear shit. The butterflies, I assume, were content, happily filling an ecological niche. My shock was a perceptual problem. I've been conditioned to associate butterflies with sympathy cards, kitchen curtains, and babies' pajamas. Butterflies are kin to sunlight, peace, and beauty and symbolize love and purity. To see them nestled on globs of glistening excrement is like bumping into Sasquatch in the backyard, or losing the Man in Red.

The world seems complicated; it's intricate, bulky, and often cryptic. Out of emotional self-defense (and sometimes pure laziness), we ever seek to simplify, generalize, and pigeonhole. This isn't all bad. If everyone passed most of their time ruminating on the nature of the universe, we'd all probably starve. Sometimes, when confronted with puzzles and nagging questions, it's wise to just say "I don't know and I don't care," then order more pizza and beer.

So far as I know ("I" being the entity that seems to reside in the cranial space immediately behind my eyes and is quite strict about empirically delineating "reality" and "dream"), I haven't actually confronted black bears with red collars that removed their heads. But: (a) A few winters ago, while skiing across a frozen lake near our home, I found a dead squirrel out on the ice. It was near the middle of the lake, far from any tree, and there wasn't a mark on the body. However, there was a short length of monofilament fishing line neatly knotted to one of the hind legs. I have a "natural" theory about this odd little corpse, but it doesn't diminish the strangeness of discovery. (b) Pieces of the planet Mars have been found on Earth. There's also a plausible theory for this unexpected notion, but what's most interesting to me is that Mars, of course, is red.

Several years ago, as mentioned, I was an enthusiastic initiate of a religious sect that unequivocally claimed to be the "one true church." After a year or two of rigorous practice in the sport of apologetics, there was no datum, image, or observation I couldn't adequately reconcile with our somewhat bizarre doctrines. This was unremarkable; the world is rife with Eric Hoffer's "true believers." What's curious is that I now snort at the dogma that consumed me (same body, same brain) for years, teachings I considered so critical to my fate and that of the entire universe that I expressed a sincere willingness to die in their behalf if necessary. I now look back and sadly chuckle at what I deem to be naive, destructive nonsense.

The circumstances that led me out of that sect are beyond the scope of this book, but it all boiled down to this: I began paying attention. I mean *paying* attention—meeting the high price (subject to continuous inflation) of brand-new, off-the-shelf, unwarped perception. It's not that I (or anyone else) can claim to have no conceptual filters or molds, but paying attention signifies that one realizes that those devices are in place.

One of my filters thoroughly screened Pam's bears and led me to believe they didn't "really exist." She presented the bears as a dream, and I accepted that interpretation so I could get out of bed and progress to my morning coffee. Naturally, if I'd had to confront the bears as Pam "saw" them, I would've seriously upset my routine, especially when they turned belligerent. (Routine whips us along more zealously than conviction.) At that hour my brain craves caffeine far more than it lusts for fresh images.

Yet here I am a month later, captivated by those red collars, spending hours writing about and around them. To say they "don't exist" has no meaning for me. And that has meaning.

8

A CHORUS OF GEESE

I t's comforting to believe that nearly everything has meaning. From nightmares to the glance of a raven, all symbolize something, and even if that symbol has meaning only to you, does that make it any less significant? Thinking is connecting, and we have the power to weave images into magic carpets of perception.

One day it was ten degrees below zero as I snowshoed across a remote northern Minnesota lake, thinking about geese. I could hear their voices in my head.

The train of thought and circumstance that led from a January ice sheet to the calls of Canada geese was this: I'd spotted a raven perched high in a Norway pine on a nearby island. It was cocking its head from side to side, and I stopped to watch. The big black scavengers possess an air of competent dignity. After all, they've been long engaged in a critical endeavor that modern Americans have only just begun to take seriously—recycling. Ravens appear to be easily, even proudly, in control. Often I've seen two or three or a half dozen on the highway, pecking at a road-killed rabbit or skunk and ignoring my car until the last instant, until my foot automatically stretches for the brake pedal. Only then will they casually hop over to the shoulder or across the centerline. I have to grin. I know that even if I tried to hit one, it would be impossible.

As I watched the raven in the pine, it suddenly squawked and dropped off the branch. It flapped a couple of times then locked into a wide, arcing glide and drifted around the point of the island. My last glimpse was of a black silhouette against gray-white overcast.

Then a deer burst out of a cedar thicket on the shore of the island. It sprinted and leapt across the ice in ravishing whitetail fashion, shooting for the mainland two hundred yards away. It was as if the raven had given some signal or warning. In a moment a second deer flashed out of the cedars, then a third. For one photographic instant all three were in view, kicking up sprays of snow as they darted in single file for the dense cover of the eastern shore. In less than a minute they'd vanished. I heard a single snap of a twig.

Had the raven indeed sounded an alert? Its parting squawk and winging shadow tripped a circuit in my brain that fetched me back three months. I thought of the autumn's first flight of geese. They had warned me about snowfields and subzero days.

"The goose honks high," people used to say when describing some auspicious event or condition. It was reference to the fact that geese fly higher in good weather. But that's not when I like to see flocks of geese.

As the autumnal equinox passes, and the sunsets bank south into the first week of October, restless currents twist through the northwest wind. The great white storms are coming. Massive Arctic cold fronts will plunge down across the border. Even the bears will seek shelter. October is a stage for lowering, leaden skies, and it's apropos to relish the lash of chilly gusts. Before the lakes and streams are sealed with ice it's fitting to watch autumn wind raising whitecaps out of gray water.

These are the days I like to hear the geese—when the clouds are close and winter seems to be burgeoning just beyond the northern horizon. The geese are honking low, and their raucous melody is a counterpoint to the tunes of cold breezes and rustling leaves. The changing of the season is one of nature's symphonies, and the calls of flying geese are written into the harmonic whole as a captivating solo.

For the geese are above it all. A silhouetted V formation skimming the fringe of a low ceiling is an outbound chorus—a transitory performance that serves as a harbinger of nature's transfiguration. You can see and hear, but you cannot touch.

There's an Amerindian creation myth that incorporates a story similar to the biblical account of the flood and Noah's ark. Evil forces have taken over the world, and a wise shaman hears a disembodied voice that warns him of the coming, purifying deluge. "When all the birds in the world," says the voice, "form up into a cloud flying from north to south, that will be the sign. Watch for the cloud of birds." The great flock duly appears, heading south, and the shaman and his wife, and "all the animals they wished to save" take refuge from the deadly rains. When the waters subside, they begin the world anew.

It's fun to speculate about the source of this legend. What more logical alarm for approaching climatic tribulation than hosts of wings driving south? The faraway calls of October geese proclaim that soon the forests will be "flooded" with snow, and humans had best take refuge from bitter winter nights.

But it's not the message itself that's so appreciated. With our technology, winter's not nearly as potent an adversary as it once was—as for the Ojibwe, who in centuries past had to survive it in the forest. What the goose song ignites is a joy that the message has been delivered. I celebrate the autumn flocks as low and swift constellations. They're like the migrating star patterns of the night sky, highlighting the season, signaling change. The lifeblood of nature is transition—from dry to green, dark to light, young to old, old to new. A zest for life arises out of variety and revision. Most people are happiest in spring and fall, when change is in the air and the freshness of the world supports a grand renewal of hope. I'm happy when I hear the geese.

For in deepest January, when the sun is muted and mornings are grim, a shadow of raven wings can remind me of October voices—and the way things change. As sure as there's ice, there'll be April. My snowshoes will again gather dust, and singing geese will head north.

9

CHICKADEE BOB

C hange, of course, can also be traumatic. Bob, for instance, lost his tail. It was on a November fourth. I remember because I was helping our friend Rastus secure his boat for the winter. It got down to nine degrees that morning, and there was a rim of ice around the lake. In two weeks there would be one great sheet, and the lake would be sealed for five months.

We dragged the sixteen-foot Lund far up onto the shore, flipped it over, and chained it to a birch. It was sad duty. The aluminum hull was crusted with frost, the anchor rope frozen stiff. Wasn't it only yesterday that the seats were warmed by June sunshine and smelled like minnows? I recalled towing a heavy stringer of small-mouth bass. But like the black bears, fishing boats must hibernate. It's just a pity they don't produce offspring while they're at it.

When we returned to the cabin, it was to a scene of high drama. Pam and I had recently begun filling our bird feeder with sunflower seeds. We do business from late October to late March, and our yard quickly becomes a hangout for jays, grosbeaks, and black-capped chick-adees. They literally flock in.

But there's a flip side to this lavish welfare program. At least once or twice a week a bird wings straight into one of our windows. We hear a loud, flat *thunk!*, and know that yet another of our clients has executed a flying body slam against the glass. I guess they're fooled by reflections of trees and sky. We rush to the window to see if there's been a casualty. Occasionally a bird is killed—usually a bigger one, such as a pine grosbeak. However, most of the time they're OK, startled and mortified, no doubt, but able to fly away from it. Some do better than others.

For instance, we still chuckle about one punch-drunk chickadee. Pam saw it hit the west window and then immediately flit over to a nearby aspen. It perched on one of the lower branches, apparently all right. But as Pam watched, it began to nod and weave. It struggled mightily to remain conscious, repeatedly jerking its little head back from the brink—as if it were last call down at the tavern. But finally the concussion triumphed. The chickadee passed out and fell forward. Pam prepared to run out and retrieve it, but the bird never left the perch. Its tiny talons had locked onto the branch, and it simply swung back and forth beneath the limb, like a feathery pendulum. It hung there for a few moments and then came to. It hoisted itself erect and flew off—a live presentation of Looney Tunes.

Well, on that chilly November morning another black-capped chickadee had pounded into a window—this one on the east side. Pam hurried to the door and found the stunned bird crouched on the top step. In another moment it would have been a quivering tidbit for The Reverend, but Pam scooped it up and brought it inside.

She cuddled it for a few minutes, afraid it was going to expire anyway. She opened her palms to take a peek, and the chickadee burst out of her cupped hands and flew wildly around the living room.

Rastus and I arrived to see Pam standing on the sofa, gingerly reaching up to where the bird had perched on a beam. Bloody Alice, our cat, was also on the sofa, watching the proceedings with great interest. Pam made a gentle thrust, but the chickadee was off, fluttering against the tops of the windows.

I grabbed Alice, and despite ill-natured protests, put her outside. I then went upstairs to the bathroom, and a moment later I heard Pam scream—and Rastus laugh. I hastened back down and found Pam clutching a small bouquet of feathers.

"Its tail came off!" she cried.

The chickadee had paused on the beam again, and instead of trying to collar the entire bird, Pam thought it would be more efficient to just pinch the tail feathers. She could then quickly cup her other hand around its pinioned body. But apparently this was an old trick used by shrikes, cats, and other predators, and the chickadee was ready with an automatic defense mechanism. It issued a loud squeak and violently beat its little wings. The tail feathers slipped out, jettisoned between Pam's fingers, and the now-stubby bird flew off.

Pam was horrified, but she finally recaptured the chickadee by throwing a dish towel over it. Tail or no, it would have to go back out into the early-winter world. But surely its tail feathers weren't expendable. We supposed this handicap would lessen its chances of survival in some way. We had read that up to 50 percent of the chickadee population dies every winter, and that in order to survive, they must feed almost constantly during the abbreviated daytime. This means a lot of flitting and flying, and presumably a raft of tail feathers is an important part of the operation. Thus, even though the chickadee flew away from the house with no apparent difficulty—and some obvious relief—we were sorrowful. Its days were probably numbered. Pam felt guilty.

And sure enough, the bird disappeared. Dozens of chickadees worked our feeder every day, from dawn till dusk, but they all had tails. We had expected the worst but were surprised the injured bird had gone so quickly. Over the next three months, as the woods filled with snow and bitterly cold air descended from Canada, Pam would often mention the hapless chickadee—regret mixed with a shred of hope. I would say, yes, it was too bad, but the bird was certainly long-dead, and that was the way of the forest, the survival of the fittest, et cetera, et cetera.

But on the morning of January 28, I heard Pam squeal, and then shout, "He's back! He's back!"

She had been watching the brisk activity at the feeder when a chickadee with no tail flew in and started pecking at the seeds. Pam was overjoyed, convinced that this was the bird whose tail she'd ripped out in November.

We immediately christened it "Bob," reflecting both its tail-less state and our strange presumption that the bird was male. I suppose we've been conditioned to associate injury, grim endurance, and survival with the males of the various species—forgetting all about pregnancy, for example. (When Pam caught herself making a chauvinistic assumption, she noted that a creature who had unwittingly dived into a closed window, and then lost its tail through an unnecessary act of bravado, was surely male.)

For the next month Bob was at the feeder almost every day, crunching seeds with the best of them. In effect he was a tagged animal, the only chickadee distinctive enough to be considered as an individual. We could follow his patterns of daily activity, unconfused by the usual isomorphic nature of chickadeehood. I had often tried to focus on a single bird, but with a dozen clones coming and going at a furious clip, I would lose track of my subject almost immediately.

But Bob stood out, and we noted that he seemed to go at the feeder in two shifts. For an hour or so each morning, and then again in the afternoon, he'd be out there hustling for seeds. Where he'd spend the rest of the working day we didn't know. Perhaps he was out eating what chickadees would naturally eat if there were no feeder. In any case, if his behavior was typical, then we were probably seeing a lot more chickadees in the course of a day than we'd suspected. For it's literally impossible to glance at the feeder at any given moment and not see a chickadee. A frenetic shift is always on duty.

At the beginning of March, Pam noticed that Bob's tail seemed to be growing back. It was becoming a little difficult to pick him out from the rest of the flock. He disappeared again, and we worried. But then, in mid-March, a chickadee zoomed in to the feeder sporting a full-length, pure-white tail. A normal black-capped chickadee's tail is gray. It had to be Bob. His resurgent feathers were a badge of honor and success; he was a hero.

We were pleased, but surprised. Back in November I wouldn't have bet a nickel on the wintertime chances of a chickadee with no tail feathers. But it was Aesop who said: "It is not only fine feathers that make fine birds."

10

AN OWL'S STARE

W hen it's extremely cold—say, forty below—
we think more about the birds. At least once
or twice each winter Pam wonders aloud
how sparrows and chickadees survive our dim season. It
adds dimension to the term *warm-blooded* to imagine
their tiny, staccato hearts versus a continent-sized polar
air mass. When I see a grosbeak perched on a bare branch,
its feathers fluffed up against relentless, killing cold, I'm
genuinely appreciative of our warm and solid house—
though I feel somewhat wimpy to be so safe and cozy
while songbirds take on winter face to face.

Our lair is hewn from native logs, and it blends into
the trees. There's no building code in our remote niche of
society, so we imitated our closest neighbors—beavers,
woodchucks, black bears—and used local materials for
our lodge.

Aspen and balsam shade our walls, and from an upstairs window we look straight into the mid-level of the
forest canopy, into the living space of squirrels, finches,
and caterpillars. In both form and function our cabin is a
tree house.

My desk faces a second-story window, and one winter
morning a blur caught my eye. I looked up to meet the
icy, unsettling stare of a great gray owl. The poplar limb
it landed on was still swaying, enhancing the hypnotic
effect of eye contact with a hunter. The huge bird was

gazing into the room, focused on my face. For an eerie moment I imagined the view from its perch, seeing a pale oval suspended in shadow behind the watery glint of glass. But the oval had a pair of eyes, and I was certain the owl would recognize them as such—wide eyes nearly as ample as its own. I wasn't prey. The round head abruptly swiveled in the better part of a full circle, a marvel of physiology that is at once comic and menacing. In another blur it dove and swooped out of sight. (Perhaps a mouse had just tunneled out of a snowdrift onto the wide plain of our buried garden.) I was pleased. The message was clear: from tree limb to tree house there was very little distance in space and time—the length of an owl's stare.

Distracted, I continued to gaze out the window, and in a moment a blue jay landed in the same tree. Beneath the long indigo tail feathers were delicate tufts of blue-gray down. I'd never noticed that before. The jay had its back to a stiff breeze and the tufts were whipped by wind— buffeted flat, then billowing out. Oblique rays of January sun, scattered through the woods, washed the jay in a spotlight of cold radiance. The sheer visual density of the illuminated down was astonishing. Why does such subtle, nearly unnoticeable beauty exist? Did God envision and design such aesthetic minutiae, or was it serendipity, a by-product of general creation? Is there provision for happy accident in the scheme of the cosmos, or are the windblown tufts of a sunlit blue jay simply accidental, period, the result of blind evolutionary chance? These propositions seem equally incredible, but my gut feeling falls within the realm of a statement by the physicist Freeman Dyson: "I do not claim that the architecture of the universe proves the existence of God. I claim only that the architecture of the universe is consistent with the hypothesis that mind plays an essential role in its functioning."

It's details that often engender the unexpected. In keeping with the tree-ness of our house we hand-split cedar shakes and nailed them to our gables as siding. They have the rough aspect of mature bark, like the shingles on the trunk of a grand old maple, and we were surprised to discover that bats love them. During the day they crawl up underneath the shakes, effectively sheltered from sunlight. Occasionally we hear them from inside the house, scratching against cedar. As voracious consumers of mosquitoes, they're welcome, and it's pleasing to know they've accepted our gables as habitat. One of our field guides reports that "some bats pass the day hanging among the foliage of trees, others hang in hollow trees," so the bats use our house as a tree. I'm flattered.

Our tree home is young. Compared to the mature balsam fir whose limbs arch toward the northwest corner of the roof, our cabin is a sapling. Judging by its girth, the fir was a seedling at the outbreak of World War I, or maybe earlier. Perhaps it passed an April night in 1910 bathed in the glow of Comet Halley. It has survived countless thunderstorms and blizzards, and at least one tornado I know of, but, most amazing, it outlived a logging operation less than twenty years ago. When we arrived, the fir was surrounded by the stumps and slash of its erstwhile neighbors—all firs of comparable size. Impressed by this tenacity, we made an effort to protect its roots as we excavated our basement—the root system of our tree house. The balsam now shields us from the punishment of northwest winds.

The loggers didn't want the birches, and these woods are generously apportioned with coppices of the stately white-trunked trees. In autumn their leaves turn gold, but it's the trunks that so richly display the spectrum. The papery bark is blank, a canvas ready for the luminous ink of sunlight. When rays slant in at dusk or dawn, filtered by atmospheric whims—haze, mist, raindrops, ice crystals—the birches are painted by vacillating wavelengths of solar radiation. It's riveting to see them all red, yellow, orange, pink, or violet against the green of the forest backdrop. It's as if a rainbow band has pierced the earth and stands upright amidst the trees. In ancient Europe birch was used for cradles because it was supposed to keep demons away. Was it because of the light and colors? Such a pure, dazzling display would be hateful to devils, and perhaps it was reasoned that the essence of brilliant color seeped into the wood.

But our house is not made entirely of trees—we also used mere lumber. I once mentioned to an acquaintance that we were building a log house, and he replied that he was, too, except that he'd had the logs sawn into two-by-fours first. We laughed, but it's more than semantics.

Trees are individuals, and no two logs are exactly the same; the forest environment promotes variation. When you build a log house, peeling, painstakingly trimming, notching, and rolling each log, surveying every one for the best fit, you quickly zero in on their uniqueness.

Trees are entities, and though we must fell some, they deserve our respect. Not only do they provide us with personal means of survival by producing fruit, watershed protection, wood, and fiber, but it has also become apparent that forests help regulate climate, and thus support all life via the maintenance of a balanced atmosphere.

Webster's defines *respect* as "a feeling of high regard, honor, or esteem." This is what I feel for trees, and though I cut several each year for fuel, I select only the diseased, or those at the end of their long lives. And I've planted more than I've felled. *Webster's* defines *to respect* as "to show polite regard by visiting or presenting oneself." I do this often. I smile at trees; I speak to them and caress them. I'm not crazy, and I'm not an animist. I simply treat the trees as well as I treat our dog and cat. I'm not alone. Recently there was an outpouring of concern for the Treaty Oak, a centuries-old giant in Austin, Texas. When someone poisoned it, the tide of human emotion rose so high that it garnered national attention. People openly wept at the sight of the sickly, partially defoliated tree. A local millionaire flew in experts to diagnose the condition. A group referred to as "New Age enthusiasts" linked hands to circle the oak and chant. It was reported that police had a suspect, and some said he should be strung up from a limb of the very tree. A tad extreme, but I understood the sentiment.

As organisms we're superior to trees in many ways. We have minds and motion (though nothing's prettier than a quaking aspen dancing in place in the wind), dreams and ambitions, and supreme power over plants and animals. Yet, as I gaze out my window into the woods I'm struck by two things: Most of the trees I can see now will still be standing when I'm buried. And if we don't nurture the remaining forests of the world, it's possible that many humans, and even entire cultures, will perish in terrible, untimely fashion. Our power may be supreme, but that of the trees may be ultimate.

In *Macbeth*, where an entire forest marches as an army, Shakespeare wrote, "Stones have been known to move and trees to speak." And their voices are pervasive. In the chatter of rustling leaves, the songs of moaning needles, and the cracking shouts of trunks on deep winter nights, I've heard their manifesto. Their motive is clear: to live and reproduce. And as they live, so do we; our lives are entwined. I know this. We're surrounded by them—by the trees that grow outside, by the logs of our cabin walls. We dream in a tree house.

11

THE TOP SECRET
STARLIGHT BRAIN

Close to a midnight one late November I was at my desk, in front of the same window the great gray owl had peered into. When I'd last checked the thermometer it was at zero; the forecast was ten degrees below. When it's that cold the atmosphere is often stable, the sky vivid. I've nurtured a passion for astronomy since youth, and before bed I intended to walk down to Secret Lake—as I do every clear night—and survey the stars, maybe see the northern lights.

Meanwhile, I was at my desk, reading. The lamp spilled a pool of light onto the book, drenching the pages with one hundred watts from a foot and a half away. The paper was stark white, like a windowpane in morning sun. I'd been there for an hour, focused on words and transported to another world by a novel. My face was warm with electric brightness. Then I switched off the lamp.

I savored the instant darkness. Except for the greenish-purple spots that drifted just inside my cornea, the blackness was total, enveloping. It was soothing after the close work of deciphering sentences. I sat still for a moment, allowing the rayless space to serve as coda to the conclusions I'd gleaned from the pages. It was like the drive home from a cinema, when the images of the screen can be filtered and polished by reality.

And there is nothing so real as blackness, nothing as tangible as nothing itself. For when the screen of your eyes goes blank, your mind is peeled back on itself, recoiled to a hub of identity. How ironic that you can hide from yourself in bright lamplight, lost in the plain open pages of a book, but you can't be concealed in complete darkness. For whatever is *you* rises immediately to the surface, pinioned by the black spotlight of nothing. Of course there must also be stillness, or your ears will quickly fill the risky void with aural information ("Quiet! I can't hear myself think"), naturally working to center your attention on the outside world, conditioned to take up the slack of eyesight. After all, the outside threats are easily understood, outside pleasures readily accessible. It's what's inside, beyond the facile grasp of the senses, that's difficult and disturbing to fathom.

I used to imagine my brain as a labyrinth of dimly lit corridors—narrow passages with filing cabinets for walls, each drawer stuffed with manila folders. Some of the folders were stamped "Top Secret," containing I guessed, the things I truly yearned to know, such as: Who is God? Why am I alive? What is the link between blue jays and spiral galaxies? How do I even know to ask? The Big Question, of course, was, Is there actually anything in those Top Secret folders? That is, was it even possible for me to have what I yearned for? Did the knowledge itself exist?

Plato would have said yes. If he were the secretary in my cerebral file room, there would be a motto from *Republic* engraved on the inside of my skull: "The knowledge at which geometry aims is the knowledge of the eternal." Because Plato figured that truth, as embodied in mathematics, has an independent existence, that humans can seek and discover it, *it* is "out there" in the universe of ideas. For example, the various mathematical formulas and theorems are all predevised and worked out, and mathematicians must simply unveil them through intellectual exercise. As Davis and Hersh wrote: "Pi is in the sky."

There is, however, another opinion. This view holds that we create truth, that mathematicians (and philosophers and theologians) develop various *models* that either work or don't work, or, most likely, fall somewhere in between—that what you get is what you see, and that what you see is often not what I see. Or, as the physicist Werner Heisenberg said, "We have to remember that what we observe is not nature in itself, but nature exposed to our method of questioning." If he were the custodian of my mental filing cabinets he would add a new folder to every drawer, boldly labeled "Other Options." And hanging from the dome of my skull would be a huge pair of fuzzy dice—the ones God plays with.

So, *is* there anything in those Top Secret folders? Who's on the payroll up there, Plato or Werner? Well, on that clear night in November I found out.

I sat still for several seconds in total darkness, and then happened to turn my head in the direction of the window. It's a two-by-four-foot pane that overlooks the forest. In daylight, from the oblique vantage point of my desk, I see young aspens and old firs reaching to the overhanging roofline of the gable, plus a good portion of the pine-board soffit. Between the roof edge and the dense foliage there's a small patch of open sky crisscrossed by aspen limbs. I'm looking southeast, and on late-autumn mornings the patch of sky is bright with sunrise. But on that moonless midnight the window was invisible. My pupils had shrunk to minimum aperture in the lamp-light, and I'd be effectively blind for several minutes, until their natural dilation resolved the night into shadows and shapes.

And yet, the instant I turned toward the imperceptible glass I saw a brilliant spark of light. It was a star, a single coruscating star. I immediately recognized Sirius, the brightest sun in the sky besides our own. I was captivated; this move had been perfectly timed. The chance tilt of my head and the direction of my inadvertent gaze had precisely coincided with the brief appearance of Sirius in that tiny limb-crowded patch of sky. Two or three minutes earlier or later, and Sirius would have been out of view.

I stared at the star. How extraordinary that it was literally all I could see. I swept my eyes from side to side, but the room and the window were completely black, and I was drawn back to Sirius as if to a vision. It sparkled like a fiery pinwheel, scintillating through the spectrum— red, yellow, green, blue, violet—like a flickering rainbow reduced to a point. I was transfixed.

Off the top of my head I knew this about Sirius: it is eight light years away, an inconceivable distance, and yet very near on the cosmic scale; it's almost twice as big as the sun, and much hotter; it shepherds a small, dim companion star that orbits it like a planet; it was highly

regarded in ancient Egypt because its annual reappear-
ance in the dawn sky at the summer solstice denoted the
rising of the Nile.

This "Sirius file" quickly flashed through my mind. I
smiled in the darkness; Sirius was an old acquaintance,
one of the first stars I'd "learned"—transferring it from
charts to memory—and this data was like personal information, as familiar as the ages and addresses of family.

And yet, what was I really seeing? My "Sirius file"
came from books; I have no direct means of discerning
the vital statistics of stars. For example, the human mind
has no fix on a "light year." It is 5,865,696,000,000 miles.
If I could race toward Sirius in a jet airliner at 600 miles
per hour, it would take 8,928,000 years to get there. I cannot "judge" that distance. It's not as if I were viewing an
earthly beacon—say a lighthouse across a bay—and was
able to gauge the possibilities in terms of hours and
miles, considering wind, waves, and the character of my
boat. I could exactly measure the water between me and
the lighthouse, envisioning in detail how the distance
would be traversed. I would *feel* how long it would
require. If an hour, that's the time from sunset to darkness, or one television drama, or about fifteen tunes on
the radio, or 5 miles traveled on my nordic skis. What is
89,280 centuries? Nothing, for all practical purposes. I
have no file for such a span that is not merely academic.
(In that amount of time, for instance, I could cover
391,046,400,000 miles on my skis—16,293,600 times
around the world.)

And so what is Sirius to my eyes—really? A pretty
light and nothing more. To call it a "star" is to be poetic.

And that's why, as I stared at Sirius, my vision flip-flopped constantly. For only a moment I saw a star, or at least my abstract notion of a distant sun. Without the context of constellations and silhouetted trees against the skyscape, it was impossible to hold the image of Sirius as Sirius.

Suddenly it was a street lamp, somebody's security light seen from a ways off. I could easily picture a neighbor in that direction. Or maybe it was an isolated yard light seen from the air. Then abruptly I was at the end of a long, straight tunnel, and far off and high up (I also saw it as a deep, deep well) was the sunlit opening; then back to Sirius for an instant, but retaining the tunnel—an unfathomable passage through space-time, and then there was a roof, a monstrous cosmic dome—the firmament—with bright light behind, a pinprick in the dome, and what if all the stars were one light that simply passes through myriad holes in a great black shell that surrounds the earth, and I was looking at one hole, but no, it seems more like a yard light again except for the dancing colors, and now it's a sparkler on the Fourth of July and I remember John holding it up in his backyard and seeing it from across the alley and the next street, or maybe it's a camper's lantern across a black lake, but no, this is Sirius and the Egyptians considered it a god, and for an instant it's a firefly in hot June darkness, but it doesn't move enough so it's back to the unreachable opening at the end of the tunnel, a fearful climb up the barrel of the well that would be worthy of a star, and yes, this is Sirius I'm gazing at, and I love the starlight in my window, through my lenses, on my retinas, into the optic nerve, and impulses to the brain—to the filing cabinets inside my skull.

And I realized those cabinets had to go. How could they contain this startling image? This is the Space Age, the New Age, the Information Age, and as my eyes slowly adjusted, I picked up the faint glow of the computer screen across the room. Photons; vibrant, domesticated. Somewhere near the computer was a small case of storage disks, electronic bins flush with words turned to ghosts and sealed in by magnetism. It was time to outfit my head with circuitry and software, with disk drives and megabytes of RAM. The manila folders were out and magic at the speed of light was in. What would Plato have thought? "Astronomy," he wrote, "compels the soul to look upward and leads us from this world to another." My visualized brain was now a new world.

This personal paradigm shift would probably have occured sooner or later anyway, even without Sirius. We re-*model* constantly, or at least we should. Does that last assertion mean that I prefer Werner over Plato? Well, if Mr. Heisenberg had seen my compact personal computer, he might have commented as he did in 1958: "Every tool carries with it the spirit by which it has been created." That definitely sounds modelish and optional, but I'd be willing to bet heavily that most individuals involved in the creation and development of computers were Platonists—they believed they'd *discovered* the necessary math and physics. I believe that too—sometimes. At other moments I yearn to know the spirits of creation, and I imagine there are many; perhaps about six billion these days.

But in those few minutes when I stared at Sirius and began replacing my filing cabinets with high-tech gear, I thought I had *it*—a new grasp of reality. My small starlight vision had been so exhilarating, so simply profound. I understood how I didn't understand understanding; I was acutely aware of awareness. However, when the transfer was done and I peered into my refurbished brain, I found that this is what it looks like now:

There are flashes of lightning coursing across the roof of my skull—a constant, arcing tapestry of long blue sparks. It's the crackle of information, feverish exchanges between pulsating disks. In the middle of this brain space, hemmed in by blinking consoles and sitting hunched over a small table, are Plato and Werner. They're playing chess. Inspired by the light snow, they play very quickly, a game every few minutes. Cries of "Checkmate!" frequently echo in the chamber—first Plato, then Werner. They beat each other all the time. Still, there is more silence than not, because although the play is fierce and precise and never stops, most of the time it winds down to: stalemate.

When, due to the spinning of our planet, Sirius edged out of the small open space amid the aspen limbs and finally disappeared, I rose from my desk. I left the house, and The Reverend walked with me down to the lake. I could see thousands of stars rimmed by tree-studded horizon. I was back in context, or in *a* context. I had to grin at the game. "Checkmate!" Stalemate. Stalemate. "Checkmate!" Stalemate. Stalemate. "Checkmate!"

Easy, boys, easy. It's all in good fun. For I suspect the matter was neatly summed up on a Saturday morning several years ago by Foghorn Leghorn, the stubborn cartoon rooster. "Oh, never mind, boy," he drawled to a precocious, smart-alecky chick. "Knowin' the answer wouldn't do me no good anyway." I believe that—sometimes. At other moments the stars convince me—getting Sirius—that all knowledge is vital and we shall live forever. Stale and mate. It's the human way.

12

FOREST GALACTICA

The stars would be less potent if not for the dark skies of our backwoods nights. Darkness is a natural resource generally unavailable to urban dwellers, and often overlooked as one of the prime attractions of rural life.

During the past several years I've noticed that some locales in our neighborhood are enhanced by nightfall, more bewitching at midnight than they are at noon. One such is the West Sturgeon Forest Road. We use it as a shortcut between our cabin and Beatrice Lake. The narrow track winds through hills full-fledged with pine and birch. Although bumpy and sometimes rutted, it leads to the center of the galaxy.

The road branches off the pavement heading northwest and never returns. Norway pines shadow a sandy grade littered with needles and cones. It's a deceptively sylvan touch, as if this were just another woodland route for loggers and hunters. Beyond the crest of the first rise, the road makes a long rolling drop to the edge of a beaver pond and then cuts due north. The pond is lost in blackness, but on warm summer evenings we catch whiffs of muskeg and peeled aspen—earthy, primeval odors, pure biology. It's a rich terrestrial habitat, but as we climb the next hill we're approaching escape velocity.

The car is aimed at the sky; we're driving to the Big Dipper. Or so it's simple to imagine. The hill's a high point, logged off and replanted eight or nine years ago. The young pines haven't yet risen to veil the horizons and crowd Polaris. It's a natural observatory—a place where a shaman could have rearranged stones to survey the solstices and the symmetry of the Great Spirit's fires.

The headlights of the car are a sacrilege, unaccountable to stones, and a manifestation of the tarnished modern magic that seeks to banish night from the planet. I switch them off before the top of the hill, and we roll to a quiet stop.

It's here that we pick up speed—when the wheels freeze and the engine dies. Silence is the trigger. We can now soar, freed from our machine, exposed to the emanations of the Milky Way. If the timing of our ascent has been blessed, we can watch the northern lights storm before the stars in waves of banshee light.

It's dark here—sixteen miles from the nearest city streetlights—uncontaminated by channeled electricity. It's a natural blind for comet hunters and lies in the path of a cosmic axis. That axis stretches from twisting infinity to a focus at the lens of imagination. In the hollow of the summer sky it is thus: At dusk the constellation Leo is "setting" in the west. It's a pleasant illusion. In reality, the planet (and our eyes) are spinning from west to east at nearly 1,000 miles per hour. The bright star Regulus, the heart of the lion, is not sinking behind the tree line. Rather, the trees are reaching to swallow it as the limb of the earth rises up and around. If you stare at the stars and watch the trees, you can sense the movement of the celestial gyros.

But this is only one facet of the cosmic maelstrom. I can recall how the hill slept in winter—a white, drifted desert under the orange gleam of Aldebaran—and I know the seasons are also the product of motion. Our forest road and all the rest are circling the sun at 66,000 miles per hour—18 miles per second—from January to July.

If I turn from Leo, face east, and then look almost straight up, I'm focused on the constellation Hercules. Our sun and its planets are racing through interstellar space toward Hercules at 43,000 miles per hour. But the solar family is also enmeshed in one of the spiral arms of the galaxy, revolving around the core of the Milky Way at 630,000 miles per hour. Velocities within velocities, orbits within orbits. And where is the galaxy going? Out. Way out to somewhere with no name.

From the top of this remote woodland hill my view of the universe is as wide as anyone's. I'm a de facto cosmologist, my own high priest and intermediary between the source of the galaxies and that part of me that is not part of my body—the potent but ephemeral mixture of perception and understanding. Some say the human mind is an epiphenomenon—it's greater than the sum of its physical parts. You cannot touch a mind, or even point to it, but at night on the West Sturgeon Forest Road, you can feel it expand.

One midnight in early June we paused on the hill and got out of the car. The Milky Way was a snowy belt of suns connecting the horizons. The constellations blazed at full power, the major patterns half-hidden by stars never seen from the hearts of civilization. It was a night for interstellar travel, with no need for a special ship.

But . . . look at the woods! The meadow of young pines was full of lights. They danced and flickered among the trees, blinking on and off like twinkling stars come to earth. Fireflies. Except for the black silhouettes of the forest, there was no difference between earth and sky. I tried to count the sparks and quit at one hundred—you might as well count the stars.

I looked up at Vega, the color of a firefly, and twenty-two light years away. I looked back at the shining zodiac of fireflies. The scale was impossible. How far to a firefly? Fifteen feet or a quantum leap? The impression of stars in the woods and insects in outer space was a near perfect illusion—like Leo "setting." The tracks of photons are relative, and the nuclear spoor of the stars resolves down to impulses in the optic nerve. Is there so little difference between stars and fireflies, between a road and the Milky Way? Perhaps it comes down to the road.

For when we cruise toward Beatrice Lake, crunching pine cones beneath the tires, we're fully aware that we're also cruising the galaxy. And so are the fireflies.

13

INSECURITY LIGHT

I'm jealous of the nighttime purity that allows me to imagine confusion between stars and fireflies, so one of these nights I'm going to load my .410 shotgun and blow away a streetlight. It'll probably be in January, when the glaring bulb is shedding harsh, third-degree illumination on falling snow. I picture the hit going down at two or three A.M. when absolutely no one is around.

Of course, there's never anyone "around" that light to begin with. For half a century the remote intersection was dark, no one deeming it necessary to light up the aspen grove and the ash swamp. But besides roads themselves, the surest harbinger of humanity's conquest of nature is the lighting of those roads. I was at the township board meeting several years ago when it was decided to install that light. A certain citizen, whom I've not seen at a board meeting before or since, insisted that for the sake of public safety a street lamp should be raised at the intersection of ———— and ————. (Since I'm going to shoot it out, it's wise to be discreet.) The board agreed to request a light from the local electric co-op. Who could oppose public safety? But afterward there were wry comments about the citizen's motives. Some said the man was less concerned about the public than he was about the fact that he often drove out from town while half in the bag, and it sure would be easier to see his turn and miss the ditch if there were a navigational beacon at the corner.

In any case, the light duly appeared, and soothing darkness was banished from another cranny of the woods (at least for the moment). The power company calls them "security lights" and seems perversely anxious to hook up as many as possible. They'll even give you a flat rate so you'll feel free to let them burn all night. Indeed, most of these lamps are actuated by photocells and automatically come on at dusk. It's a curious practice in this modern age of conservation and a possible greenhouse effect. As more people move out from town to live in our remote, backwoods township, "security lights" blaze the trail, and rare is the newcomer who can resist the impulse to bathe his property in electric mist and make his homestead look as much like a city address as possible. Why?

They're god-awful bright, but where's the security? If I were prone to robbery, the houses I'd attempt to sack would be those lit up and advertised by "security lights." How better to discover: Is there a Doberman sleeping on the porch? Where did the kids leave the wagon, the basketball, the tricycle, or anything else I might trip over? Is there anything outside worth stealing? Are any windows unlocked? And so on and so on. The light would be a boon, and there would still be plenty of deep shadows to mask my approach. (Made all the deeper by contrast.) I would hate to sneak into a pitch-black yard. Indeed, why risk it if the neighbor is dumb enough to keep his lighted?

When I was a small child, I insisted on sleeping with a lamp on in my room. I was afraid of the boogeyman, but finally consented to sleep in darkness when a friend convinced me that the light only allowed the boogeyman to get a better look at me. Our security lights are symbols of fear and distrust—of one-sided notions of night as evil and menacing. It's true that darkness can conceal, but it's also liberating and revelatory. If our portion of the planet were never in shadow, our cosmos would consist of a minuscule patch of sunlit earth; we'd be unaware of star clusters and galaxies, ignorant of the wondrous expanse of the universe. Our perspective would be fully illuminated, but painfully small. Are we afraid of open space? Is that why so many deliberately seek to destroy the night, even when they have no actual reason to expect the predations of muggers, thieves, or prowlers? Even when a backwoods intersection is more than adequately plumbed by the headlights of our vehicles? What need is there to shed constant light on a stretch of road that is vacant 99 percent of the time? Our reasons must transcend practicality and reach for a deeper fear. And, at least in these woods, it's time to get over it. "In a dark time," wrote Roethke, "the eye begins to see."

Because in the darkness is a new world, a planet turned away from its star, where the multitude of daylight images and distractions are tempered by shadow. We can know the heavens only at night, outdoors, as our pupils gradually expand to let in the cosmos.

Several years ago, I was a Bible college student in Texas, and one day we were lectured on the Book of Ecclesiastes. The instructor waxed verbose concerning the first chapter and its philosophical statements about the human condition, and he settled with enthusiasm on verse nine: " . . . and there is nothing new under the sun." I glanced at the young woman in the seat beside me, who was hunched over her Bible, carefully writing in the margin next to verse nine. When she finished, I leaned over and read: "But what about the rest of the universe?" Indeed. And explorations of that require darkness.

Back in the sixties, Simon and Garfunkel had a smash hit with their song "The Sounds of Silence." The opening line is: "Hello darkness, my old friend. / I've come to talk with you again." It suggested a communing with the night that I found irresistible, and it quickly became my favorite song. There's no greater stimulus to reflection than strolling down a country road under a dark sky with constellations blazing beyond a foreground of trees. I feel less the pure earthling and more a citizen of the galaxy; I sense the reality of space-time, anointed in starlight that has traveled for centuries and millennia. I feel more powerful—not overwhelmed by the bright clamoring of a sunstruck afternoon. With the mellowing of visual cues, I seem to hear more clearly. The night, particularly in summer, oscillates with the grand noise of life, responding to the regime of darkness. Most of these impressions and sensations are simply ruined by gluts of artificial light. As Paul Simon sang: "And the people bowed and prayed / To the neon god they made."

I'll grant that a yard light is handy occasionally, but I've never understood why people just don't employ them as needed. Once old Aunt Hattie has safely negotiated the icy walk from her car to the back door, just switch the damn thing off. The owls don't need it, and your neighbors don't want it. Why move into the bush (and it's more newcomers than old-timers), where one of the chief advantages is an awesome, star-studded night sky, and then blot out the natural nocturnal peace with energy-sucking, artificial (and cold) electric light pollution? It's decadent, ignorant, and unbecoming of adults. We should all realize by now that boogeymen are not afraid of night-lights, and anyway, you left most of the goblins behind in the city.

Much is made of water pollution—by both organic and inorganic compounds—and rightly so. But light can pollute a lake as readily as sewage or mercury. Fifteen years ago I could sit on the shore of Little Sturgeon Lake and note two or three security lights along the far shore. The night wasn't pristine, but neither was it broken. Now, especially in summer, the shore is girdled with security lights, and the once-dark water is stabbed and criss-crossed with two dozen interfering reflections, resembling some traffic-choked metropolitan harbor. With that much careless light dumped into the lake, can sewage be far behind? The mindset that pollutes, whether with light or physical wastes, is the same.

I once saw a photo of a satellite-eye-view of North America at night, and I was stunned. Even from 20,000 miles the continent is splotched with vast seas of light. It has deteriorated to the point where some astronomical observatories have been effectively hobbled by man-made daylight—glaring, starscape-killing grids of millions of bulbs. I'll concede that it's desirable to illuminate city thoroughfares that never cease to hum with traffic, but our current levels of lighting are as much a product of our once-cheap energy as of a need to see at night ("We can afford to do it, so why not?"). We're wasting light. For example, at the urging of the astronomical community, the board of supervisors of Coconino County, Arizona, which includes Flagstaff, and the Lowell and U.S. Naval Observatories passed an ordinance in 1989 that limits the quantity of light that can be shed on each acre of land. To help convince the county to pass it, the astronomers conducted a detailed photometric study of Flagstaff and discovered that by merely shielding and properly aiming existing lights, lower wattage could be used to achieve the same degree of illumination. Local government and business will realize financial benefits from the ordinance. One hopes they'll also enjoy the darker skies.

There are no observatories in our township, so I can't appeal to a local sense of responsibility for astrophysical research. I can only say to the light junkies: (a) Use light only when you need it. You won't save money, unfortunately (that archaic, sinful flat rate), but you will save energy and thereby be more environmentally responsible; think globally, act locally. (b) Check out the beauty and benefits of moonlight, starlight, and the northern lights. Once your eyes adjust, you won't need a mercury-vapor fix (and the boogeyman won't see your German shepherd until it's too late). (c) Since the lamp at ———— and ———— will soon be gone, there are some of you who should drink at home. (d) After I work up the nerve to shoot one lamp, I'm sure the vivification spurred by rebellion will cause the next shot to come easier. And beware, I know where all the lights are.

14

DANCING GHOSTS

S ilence is power. A shout or a shot will turn your head, force a reaction, but loudness is superficial—an obvious manifestation that's readily deciphered. Silence, however—the absence of vibration—is mysterious. We're drawn to quiet things, deliberately plumbing the frequencies of stillness. We're compelled to listen to whispers, and silence is strong.

One reason mankind has always been fascinated by the night sky is that there's light, movement, and pattern, but no sound. Sky is where science and religion meet, each speaking for voiceless stars. The passion to know, to believe, is often ignited by the strangeness of the sky. And in that sky there's nothing more bizarre, more tantalizing, than the polar lights. When the night erupts with auroral magic, what happens? Not just to ions, but to our minds?

An aurora begins at the core of the sun. The gravitational force of the sun's mass exerts horrific pressure on hydrogen atoms, and they fuse to produce a new element, helium. Four hydrogen atoms are transformed into one helium atom. Strangely, the mass of the helium atom doesn't equal four hydrogen atoms, it's a little less. This tiny difference in mass is spewed out as energy, that is, light and heat; or so it's believed. The sun shines.

In addition to visible light and other radiation, the sun broadcasts charged atomic particles. This emission is the "solar wind." The particles whip through space at millions of miles per hour, and it's the pressure of this "wind" that tugs at comets and creates their tails. Theory says this stream of particles lashes the earth's upper atmosphere—50 to 400 miles up—where molecules of nitrogen and oxygen divide into single atoms. The particles of the solar wind, barreling in from the sun after a day of interplanetary travel, collide with these atoms and excite them. This causes the air to glow in a wild electrical storm. Charged particles are sucked into the atmosphere around the polar regions because of the concentration of the planet's magnetic field, and the glowing is therefore magnified around the poles. In the north, the aurora borealis bursts into vibrancy. In the Southern Hemisphere it's called the aurora australis.

This esoteric speculation is a shade less romantic than the folk tale that says the northern lights resulted from the hullabaloo raised by Paul Bunyan and Babe the Blue Ox while wrestling for fun at the North Pole.

Aurora was the Roman name for the goddess of dawn, hence *aurora borealis* may be literally translated as "northern dawn." And so it seems, as the north horizon glows with celestial twilight in the midst of night. This polar "dawn" can have an eerie impact.

On March 23, 1969 (I'll never forget it), at about seven-thirty in the evening, I happened to glance out our bedroom window. I'm startled by the northern lights; they always seem strange. But that night I was astounded. The entire northern sky was writhing with rays and arcs. The aurora was a rich, blazing emerald green, the brightest I'd ever witnessed. It extended toward the zenith, out of my range of vision. I ran through the house to a south window and gasped. The southern sky was inflamed by a brilliant red curtain—fantastic, surreal. Euphoric, I rushed from window to window, unwilling to tear my eyes away from the show long enough to get dressed and dash outside. Never had I seen such vivid colors in the night sky. From horizon to horizon the heavens were a green and red tapestry in a dynamic state of flux, an awesome riot of celestial chaos. It was overwhelming beauty. It was a dance of sky spirits, conjured out of emptiness and leaping madly to the melody of cold silence.

In a few minutes it was over. The inscrutable stars hung silent and steady; our windows stood clear and blank. My lips uttered prayers.

Apocalyptic visions come to life on nights when even the stars are dimmed behind red and green sheets of scintillating light. The firmament is afire, bringing dreams and delusions to poets and prophets.

The Roman historian Livy wrote of a display in 464 B.C.: "The heavens were seen to blaze with numerous fires, and other portents were either actually seen or were due to the illusions of the terror-stricken observers. To avert these alarms, a three-days session of prayer was ordered."

The northern lights were rare in Rome, and hence naturally startling, but even in parts of the world where displays were more frequent they were regarded as ominous. In *Suns, Myths, and Men*, Patrick Moore writes, "Like comets, auroras were regarded as signs of ill fortune, and the idea still lingers on in parts of north

Scotland where the Lights are known as 'the Merry Dancers.' And looking back to 12 January 1570, we find a description of an aurora which was so bright that 'no such gruesome spectacle had been seen or heard of within living memory.' The writer went on: 'Wherefore, dear Christians, take such terrible portents to heart and diligently pray to God, that He will soften his punishments.' "

The Ojibwe translation of aurora borealis is "dancing ghosts." Instinct tells us that with all this light and motion there should be sound. As with thunder and lightning, there should be some auditory handle to help us pinpoint and define the disturbing light. We know lightning because we know thunder. We know they go together with rain, and so, obviously, did primitive men. But the aurora goes with nothing. It materializes on a particular night for no apparent reason. It performs a ghostly dance, sometimes mimicking the color of blood. That many peoples considered it a reason for prayer is no surprise. And yet, how comforting to "see" your ancestors dancing with the stars.

The frequency of auroral displays seems to be linked to the sunspot cycle. Sunspots are temporary "cool" areas that appear as black patches on the sun's disk. They possess strong magnetic fields and are thought to be a major factor in the appearance of solar flares. Flares are high-intensity "flames" of energy that extend thousands of miles out from the sun. They cause an increase in the volume of solar winds, and hence in the frequency of auroral activity. The peak of sunspot influence occurs on an average of every eleven years, and during this peak the northern skies often blaze with a maximum of auroral activity.

It was recently discovered that the Van Allen radiation belts—revealed in 1958 by the first U.S. satellite, *Explorer I*—may also affect the frequency of auroras. The belts of subatomic particles extend from 400 to 40,000 miles above the earth and partially shield us from the solar wind. "Overflows" and "leakages" of electrons from the outer belt are probably the immediate source of auroral displays. The influence of the Van Allen region may explain why significant sunspot activity doesn't always trigger an aurora, and why the time lag between sunspots and auroras is unpredictable.

The annual seasonal maximums of auroral storms occur during the equinoctial months of September/October and March/April. This is because the tilt of the earth's orbit causes it to be more directly in line with the highly active polar areas of the sun. So the best time to observe the northern lights is within a few weeks either side of the equinoxes—the first day of spring and the first day of autumn. As an attempt to keep touch with cycles and seasons, I maintain records of several phenomena. Over the past twenty-three years (1966–69 and 1975–93), I've observed 681 auroral displays from northern Minnesota. (The average is 29 auroras per year, or 2 to 3 displays per month.) I live at forty-seven degrees, forty minutes north latitude, and that's near the southern edge of regularly observed auroral activity. Below forty degrees north latitude the northern lights are rare. Even in the Minneapolis-St. Paul area—at forty-five degrees, halfway between the equator and the pole—the northern lights are seen significantly less than they are up here. But we're fortunate in North America because we're much closer to the north geomagnetic pole (where compasses actually point) than are Europeans or Asians. This pole—where auroral activity is centered—lies in northern Canada, so we generally see more displays than folks at similar latitudes on other continents. It also helps to have a dark, rural skyscape. Many displays aren't bright, and some are little more than faint, amorphous glows on the northern horizon. Urban light pollution and haze can easily mask an aurora.

A prediction that panned out spectacularly was the one touting 1989–90 as a solar maximum period with increased flare activity on the sun, and hence more auroral disturbances. I saw 69 displays in 1989 and 63 in 1990 (in February alone I saw 15—a record for one month), many of them unusually wild and colorful. (In the spring of '89, some displays were seen as far south as the Carolinas.) My previous annual record was 39, in 1978. Since November 1990, the rate of auroral activity has been returning to normal, though some solar flare activity in the spring of 1991 caused outstanding displays for a few weeks, and an auroral storm can appear at any time.

Even though I can expect to view the northern lights every other week, it's a spectacle that's never dull. Like snowflakes, each display is different. I've seen every color of the spectrum and mixtures thereof; I've seen patterns so swift and tangled they boggle the mind. There are five basic auroral states: rays, glows, flames, rayed arcs (or curtains), and crowns (or coronas), and they often blend to form grand, livid mosaics that seem to kindle the sky.

On the evening of November 8, 1991, a friend and fellow aurora enthusiast phoned me from south of Milwaukee (latitude forty-two degrees). He was breathless.

"Get outside!" he commanded. "There's an incredible display."

"Bummer!" I replied. "It's overcast here."

I went out anyway, hoping perchance it might clear. It didn't, but the low clouds were thin, and I noticed a strange pulsation. I stared. The aurora was so bright I could see it *through* the overcast. As my eyes adjusted to the night I noticed the clouds were tinged with a pale red glow and seemed to be writhing and rolling even though there was no wind. It was like watching a fire behind smoked glass, and I could only speculate how powerful the display must be.

At first I was disappointed—what lousy timing for cloud cover. But then this more subtle glory asserted itself. Because of the overcast, the entire atmosphere seemed to be ablaze. Only partially seen, the aurora was thus made even more visible, firing the imagination as well as the sky. Dancing ghosts indeed.

15

THE VIRIDIAN GATE

G hosts do more than dance, and they aren't restricted to nocturnal visits. I once contemplated 30,000 of them in the grand luminosity of a summer sunset mirrored in Secret Lake.

When The Reverend and I first arrived at the shore that evening, we saw the island was back. It was nestled against our dock, pinned by a gentle southeasterly breeze. I hadn't seen it for a month.

The island is roughly seven feet on a side and about two-and-a-half feet thick. It's a durable mat of muskeg, supporting a lush verdure of labrador tea, leatherleaf, pitcher plants, cranberry vines, and sphagnum moss. It roams Secret Lake with the wind, occasionally passing a day or two bumping the poles of our tiny pier—like a moored boat. It's a little world on waves, independent of its bog mother; a chunk of shoreline that somehow broke free several years ago. My theory: a large bull moose ambled too near the edge of the floating muskeg and ripped through. As he lunged and thrashed, finally kicking into open water and swimming away, the island was torn loose. It continues to thrive, a mobile ecosystem that goes with the flow.

I've portaged a lawn chair down to the dock this evening, and as I unfold it, The Reverend leans out to sniff at the island. He's half Lab, and it's been a bad day for a black dog—sunny and in the high eighties. He spent the afternoon panting under the back porch, and though fond of the lake he doesn't come down alone. He used to enjoy the water more before his accident. One day he was hanging far over the edge of the dock, peering at something in the water, when his front paws let go and he plunged nose-first. He sank like a waterlogged beaver cutting, vanishing completely; a gulp of bubbles broke the surface. After a long moment he burst out of the depths, snorting and wild-eyed, paddling in panic for shore. Dogs are good swimmers but only inadvertent divers. He shook and coughed and wouldn't set foot on the dock again that day. Now it must be scorching hot before he'll go in.

After a cautious olfactory sweep, The Reverend hops onto the island and starts shoving his snout into the moss. Something's caught his attention, and he's unfazed by the quaking of the mat. I consider giving the island a push and sending The Rev for a ride, but it's been a long day and I ease into the lawn chair instead. I'll settle for more subtle entertainment than a surprised, betrayed dog.

It's a few minutes past nine, and the solstice sun has just set. We'll have a luxurious hour of June twilight, and if the mosquitoes don't drive me off, I'll watch some lingering cumulus clouds stained into rainbows—one color at a time, until the stars take over. I'm eager to see the most enlightening shade, the delicate blend of yellowish blue-green that tints the western horizon at deep dusk. Vega and Altair will already be winking in the east, and this resonant hue will endure only a few minutes. A good thing, for it's much too beautiful. It's the color of goddess eyes, a reflection of eternity. If I could leave this planet at will, rising up in a quantum leap, that narrow band of viridian would serve as the gate to another universe.

In the meantime we've got action. A solitary loon offers a tremolo to the air, and it strums my spine. She's just twenty yards from the dock. She? Only an expert could determine loon gender at that distance, but the call struck me as feminine—sirenlike, yet soft and virginal. She breaks into a long performance of rapturous yodels, and in the enhanced silence that follows I'm startled by a whoosh directly overhead. Another loon is banking over the dock—wings spread wide, feathers splayed—"flaps down" as it were. The sound is identical to that of a landing aircraft in the moment when the Doppler effect has sent the engine noise the other way, and you can clearly hear the sigh of wings. With my eyes closed there'd be little difference between Cessna and loon. It's amusing how technology imitates biology, but what could be more natural?

The loon curves into the breeze and drops at a steep angle, neck up, canting almost perpendicular to the water before its tail hits, gracefully ruddering its torso into an extended splashdown as wings are folded into the amphibious mode. The transition from flying to swimming is as smooth as synchromesh and is greeted with a single high note (appreciative?) from the female. The loons immediately begin preening and fishing, and it occurs to me that the island would provide an excellent nesting site for them—if it weren't so vagrant. Most creatures get tense when their eggs go roaming.

Above, I notice the bright contrail of an airliner; a 727 I suppose, still lit by the sun I can no longer see. The vapor is dyed orange—a cloud created by jet engines, and for a moment I'm on the verge of another biology-technology analogy. But a beaver slaps its tail not ten yards away, and I almost spill my beer. The Rev leaps back onto the dock, ears perked, tail rigid. Old Castor has snuck up on us again.

The beavers moved in five years ago, raising a lodge on the northern shore. It's true, they stay busy. Three or four have virtually clear-cut five acres of aspen and birch—pretty amazing when you're using your teeth and you waddle on land (and work only the night shift and take winters off). Last autumn I planned to drop a log across the stream that flows out of Secret Lake. I enjoy walking that way, and it would serve as a crude, low-impact bridge. No need. When I hiked over I discovered the stream no longer existed. The compulsive beavers had replaced it with a hundred-foot-long dam. So, that's why the lake level rose all last summer.

What intrigues me (and The Rev) about the beavers is that they always approach the dock. One or two will swim over when we arrive and cruise back and forth in front—sometimes a mere ten feet away. I can see their pupils and hear them breathe. Periodically they slap and dive, but nobody seems terribly excited. I assume this promenade is a defensive measure, perhaps a warning; and sure enough, The Rev and I never assault beavers or pilfer aspen cuttings.

However, I have toyed with the idea of climbing a-board the island and paddling it to the vicinity of the beaver lodge during the day. I'd half burrow into the moss, then cover myself with fresh aspen limbs. When the beavers emerged at dusk, I'd try to pat one on the head when it came over to check out the aspen. It would be "counting coup"—gentle revenge for all the times I've been startled by tail slaps.

There's only one beaver this evening, and The Reverend quickly loses interest. The first time he saw one near the dock he jumped in. But the beaver vanished, and I yelled, and that was the end of it. He's still fascinated, but only for one minute at a time.

A pair of mallards zip by at spruce-top level—quacking—and Rev looks up, but he's ready to return to the house. He's truly a domesticated animal. On the other hand, his nose has probably told him all he needs to know about the lake this evening, and it's likely he's gleaned more information than I have. But he won't leave alone.

I'm hoping we'll hear The Screamer; that would keep the dog interested. For the past fifteen years we've regularly heard an awful squawking-keening at night—more often than not from the direction of the lake. It drives The Reverend crazy. He growls and barks and charges off into the woods with hackles high. Our previous dog reacted the same way. In fact, other than trespassing ATVs, it was the only thing that ever upset him. I assume The Screamer is a bird, since it seems to travel so fast. Is it an owl? I imagine I could find out with a little research, but it's more fun to leave it enigmatic. Still, I'd be thrilled to actually see a creature generate that hair-raising cry.

Maybe if I spent a night on the dock or, better yet, on the island.

Hearing The Screamer would be appropriate this evening, because one reason I've come down to the lake is that I'm disturbed. I need the therapy of water and twilight. It was nothing specific at first, but now I keep focusing on a news item I heard on the radio. There's been a major earthquake in Iran, and it's reported that more than 30,000 people have died—many of them horribly, no doubt. But, of course, for the dead it's over, the pain is done. Many thousands more are still alive—bereaved, homeless, utterly shocked. Some have probably gone insane, their world literally shattered. It's the island that keeps me thinking of them.

Rather, I saw the mat of muskeg and the word *island* came to mind. That led me to recall the once-profound, now-cliché words of the preacher John Donne: "No man is an *Island*." And I was forcefully struck by the apparent. Those humans in Iran—news items—really exist. If I headed for that band of blue-green sky (a mere 727 would do), I could be with them in a few hours. It's not another universe; they're just around the curve of the globe, and we share the same atmosphere. We're linked, and their suffering disturbs me. "Any man's *death* diminishes *me*," wrote Donne.

And yet it's astonishing that I can sit in my lawn chair, relaxing with loons and beavers, scratching the ears of a beloved dog, and being mesmerized by a kaleidoscopic sunset. How can I be so blessed, the Iranians so cursed, at the same time on the same planet? Is simple distance that potent? Apparently. For I also recall a saying from the Talmud: "Every man has the right to believe that just for him was the world created." I'm privileged; this light and these animals are mine. Death belongs to the far-away, unfortunate Iranians.

And here is the paradox: we are not islands; we are indeed islands. Both. I'm the only human on the lake, but the sunset glows for millions. I'm a wandering island—touching here, bumping there. The big question, of course, is, Where did I come from? I trust I was not set afloat by a careless bull moose. Nor by any other accident. I like to fancy there's salvation beyond that viridian gate. Perhaps we'll make the quantum leap someday. Perhaps 30,000 Iranians have just done it. Meanwhile, a donation to the Red Cross for earthquake relief is as good as anything.

Before I leave the dock, I give the island a shove. It's time for it to touch somewhere else. The Reverend sprints for the house. It's been a bad day for a black dog.

16

THE NEW MOON OF THE DEEP SNOW

The Reverend isn't fond of high summer or deep winter. In July he hunkers under the back porch, viciously nipping at horseflies. In January he curls into a furry lump on the kitchen rug, pointedly ignoring me as I slip on boots and parka, grimly aware that I may order him outdoors as partner to whatever idiotic human mission I may have in mind. The Rev seems happiest in spring and fall, when temperatures are moderate and most of his insect tormentors are slow, dead, or unborn.

For me, however, the delicious extremes of the northern temperate zone are one of its joys. I'm delighted that the summer high temp and the winter low can be 150 degrees apart; that even in January a high-low span of 90 degrees is not unusual; that a lush green and growing July becomes pure white and glassy, passing through red, orange, and yellow in between. I even like it that our long driveway, frozen as solid as Jovian moons for five months, mutates to warm mud in April.

The difference in ambience from the summer solstice to the winter solstice approaches the epic, like a journey between planets—June on Venus, December on Mars. Many prefer the June edition of the solstice with its noisy carnival of life and reign of benevolent sunlight. The last month of the year can be too cold and bleak, and newspaper obituary columns always seem lengthy around

Christmas. But even bleakness arrives with a sessile pati-
na of natural magic, and I'm a firm believer in the effica-
cy of winter as a therapist. Parturient silences and clean
landscapes offer a promise of fresh beginnings, and if certain hopes lie dormant it's only because they're gathering
strength.

The glories of bleakness are mostly subtle, but occasionally they can also be spectacular. One December
afternoon I stopped my skis and sighed; leaned on the
poles and gazed across frozen Secret Lake. It was no sorceress that cast this spell upon the country, but the
results were no less bewitching. All that I viewed—forest, lake, sky—was minted in lustrous shades of gray,
from almost pitch dark to nearly pure light. The scene
was like the emulsion on a grand, surreal black-and-
white negative, inscribed in 3-D silver.

From my ski tips outward, the wind-polished snowfield of the ice sheet, slightly blurred by its blankness,
was master of ceremonies to the forest beyond. The
black spruce on the far shore were limned with hoarfrost,
each twig and needle glazed with pearly ice. Up close the
rime looked like feathers or fur, building and branching
like crystalline cacti, the patterns ever more intricate.
From a distance the spruce were ghost trees, ethereal and
majestic. Behind them the land sloped up from bog, and a
sheltered stand of fir and spruce appeared as black spires,
limbs uncoated and lucid, highlighting the yet loftier
woods of aspen and birch that were frosted to an opales-
cent gray-white canopy beneath a bright elliptical patch
of sky resembling a halo, or an eerie auroral glow. I knew
this halo was "iceblink," a reflection on the overcast of

the other lake beyond the trees. The rest of the sky was an inscrutable metallic gray, low enough to seem solid.

This winter virtuosity—overwhelming yet delicate, potent but fragile—was almost arctic in its presence and loneliness. Such manifestations of crystal aren't rare in northern Minnesota, but they're usually fleeting. A warm, relatively humid afternoon is followed by a cold, dry night, and by dawn the forest is a fairyland—for a few hours. Sun and wind devour the frost before noon. But that year was different.

On the day after Christmas the hoarfrost appeared, but there was no sun or appreciable wind—for nine days. A vast bubble of stable air settled over the region and weather forecasts became monotonous mantras. For more than a week the temperature hovered between twenty-five and thirty degrees, day and night; the barometer was a metronome, pegged at just over thirty inches, the needle tracing a tiny diurnal arc. The jet stream flowed far to the north, and during a span when it should have been well below zero at night, and not much warmer by afternoon, the eaves began to drip.

Fed by moist air and morning fog, the crystals shrouding the forest burgeoned. Each day was more enchanting than the last, and the vitreous spears and shards, ever merging, extended as much as two inches from their bases of needles and twigs.

Each day I keenly anticipated sunlight. Out on my skis I tried to imagine how the haunting landscape would appear if the billions of crystals were flooded with light, refracting, reflecting, like a galaxy of chipped diamonds, and all against the backdrop of blue sky. I was certain that if the sun were to suddenly breach the overcast and charge these latent optics with photons, I'd burst into tears. In grays, the beauty was aching—how to touch it? how to drink it in?—in the pomp of full sunlight it would be too much, like an explosion so loud and bright that the senses cannot totally register the impact.

On the afternoon of New Year's Eve it almost happened. I was skiing through an old clear-cut, a twenty-five-acre opening in the forest now studded with pine saplings, when the snow suddenly waxed to a paler shade of white-gray. I stopped and looked at the sky. For the first time in five days there was definition to the clouds. A freshening southwesterly breeze was tugging at the overcast, and for a tantalizing minute I saw a bright smudge where clouds thinned before the sun. This is perfect, I thought, I'm in a natural arena, in the middle of a clearing surrounded by frosted trees. I braced for the glittering fire of sunbeams, prepared to shout with the joy of sensual overload.

But no. Although the wind increased, the clouds rethickened, and the smudge of brightness faded back into a uniform shade of steel gray. I resumed skiing and glided into a stand of jack pine, which was still crystallized, still the somber tone of deep winter. And the tension built; when would the sun ignite the world? I longed for it.

That memorable winter began on Halloween, when the first flakes of a vast blizzard started falling just after dark. Meteorologists called it a "megastorm," and by November 2, when it tapered off to flurries, it had dumped more than three feet of snow on Duluth. We got seventeen inches, and a colder-than-normal November plus another foot of snow by Thanksgiving ensured that the land stayed white. Secret Lake froze over on November third, and we had our first subzero night on the fourth. The winter had arrived angry and howling, smothering autumn forthwith and for good. It caught most everyone by surprise, and our canoe was buried down on the lakeshore, frozen to the ground. As I struggled to free it and then portage up to the house through thigh-deep drifts, I was bemused by the notion of switching from paddles to ski poles in a matter of hours. I was ready for skiing, but this was going to be an exceptionally long season.

And then came the strange late-December spell of moisture. I likened the overcast to the dead weight of the waning old year. How appropriate it would be for the sun to return on January first, christening the new year with a flash of brilliant promise. But on New Year's Day it was still cloudy, and the temperature crept up to thirty-six degrees. The breeze was warm and it smelled like March. The hoarfrost began to disintegrate, wafting to the ground in flurries of translucent chips. At night, the mercury barely dropped below freezing, and I felt cheated. The frost wouldn't re-form, and I decided that even if it meant temperatures of thirty- or forty-below, let the jet stream plunge south, let cold clear air sweep the clouds away. Picture this wonderland in moonlight! Imagine the lunar glow magnified by a billion tiny mirrors. But nothing changed.

On January second it was thirty-four degrees, on the third it was thirty-three, and by the end of that day all frost had vanished. The grayness and white were no longer beguiling and potentially vivid; all had eroded to dampness and murk.

On the fourth it was sunny. Sure! I thought, now that the remarkable hoarfrost is gone. I chuckled, realizing I was actually bitter about it. Not that the day wasn't seductive. The temperature rose to thirty-eight degrees and I skiied more than ten miles in theraputic sunshine —I couldn't stop, couldn't bear to be indoors. I watched the sunset over Secret Lake, and the oblong winter twilight culminated in a radiant band of red-orange that faded into yellow and blended with the blue-violet of descending night. Vega twinkled in the northwest, dipping for the horizon. How fine to see a star.

When I'd checked my calendar that morning I saw we were at the dark of the moon; there would be no lunar glow to enrich this first clear night in almost two weeks. I noted that according to Native American reckoning it was the New Moon of the Deep Snow, and an image surfaced: A wigwam or teepee half buried in drifts, a tendril of smoke rising from the top, and inside a family huddled together in buffalo robes and bearskins. They know there's much winter remaining, and other dark moons— New Moon of the Crusted Snow, New Moon of the Snowshoe Breaking. The faces I see in the wigwam are grim.

And that, I know, is the traditional face of winter. In this modern era I enjoy the luxury of feeling cheated by ephemeral hoarfrost. I'm not often threatened by winter, merely enthralled. That's true progress, real wealth. My fortune is measured by the number of miles that pass beneath my skis; my luck is a windfall of sunlight, and a particular phase of the moon.

The rest of the winter was more typical, until February 29—Leap Day, which is unusual by definition. It was six below zero that morning but rose to a bright and vernal forty-one by late afternoon. Coupled with sunshine that actually warmed the skin, it was the first breath of a suddenly possible spring. It had been a long haul since Halloween.

Just before sunset our friend Harold phoned to say he'd lit his sauna and had a pot of chili on the stove, and Pam and I were invited to share both. No coaxing was necessary, and we promptly drove to the end of Greenrock Road and parked our car next to a slowly collapsing snow drift. The effect of the sun was evident and cheering.

Harold lives on an island in Big Sturgeon Lake, and we hiked a couple of hundred yards across the ice to his sauna. The chimney was belching only heat waves. A robust fire was well along, promising that most precious of northern winter commodities—steam.

Harold likes to heat up about fifty gallons of water in the "boiler" he set up in the sauna, and my job was to fill it. He handed me a freshly sharpened ice chisel and some buckets, and I walked out a few paces beyond the dock where he'd cleared a patch of snow from the ice. Enjoying the surprising efficiency of the heavy chisel, I began chopping healthy chunks out of the lake.

The ice was about two feet thick, tinted a translucent blue-green—Arctic gemstone—and it was like chipping glass. With the sun just below the horizon, a wide swath of cirrus cloud was suffused with pinkish light. Male ice, female sky, and where they merged a band of yellow-orange at the treetops. Jupiter was rising—a spark of white fire over the jack pines on the mainland. I had a sense of posing for some unseen photographer or painter as the snow was stained the color of dusk. I leaned on the chisel for a moment and spun slowly in a circle, not merely looking, but *willing* the color into my eyes, consciously packing them with light. It's not enough for eyes to be open; they have to be switched on as well, and I imagine vision as powered by electricity, the current generated by waves sucked through the iris and splashed onto the retina. Acute vision requires effort, though it's a pleasant kind of work.

And so was chopping ice. I easily carved a hole large enough to dip a bucket, and when I broke through, water surged up to fill it, like the fountain of an artesian well.

Using four pails, Harold and I set up a short relay. I filled two buckets and carried them to the dock. He took them and handed me two empties. As he hauled the pails into the sauna and dumped them into the boiler, I fetched two more, and thus we shuttled for several minutes like a pair of motivated beavers. Part of the charm of a wintertime sauna is that earnest preparation is required, and value thereby added.

It was fully dark when we entered the sauna, which is lit only by a kerosene lamp. The night was going to be cold, but inside Pam was delighted to read the ther-

mometer up in the corner—190 degrees. Harold dashed
the piping rocks with a ladle of water, and steam roiled
up to envelop us in life-affirming mist. If music could be
created in sinus cavities, mine would have composed a
bouncy jazz number.

After the mandatory ritual of ooohs, aaahs, and "this is
living"s, we settled into desultory conversation, minds
and tongues relaxed. Sauna discussions can be particularly fruitful because they're secondary to the steam and
less important than the aaahs. Ideas are in, wrangling is
out; it demands too much energy and seems incongruent
in such a congenial (and fleeting) environment.

General observations about warmth versus chill led to
talk about dinosaurs (recent study indicates that many of
them were warm-blooded) and to their possible extinc-
tion via a catastrophic asteroid impact sixty-five million
years ago. This train of thought ended with a critique of
Darwinism and the newer theories of evolutionary
change. It was election year '92, and we moved on to the
demagoguery of Pat Buchanan, the trials of Bill Clinton
(who seemed like a real long shot just then), and something about loan guarantees to Israel.

That closed the first shift and we shuffled out the door
into the bracing cold of Leap Day night. We sat on a
bench and steamed like cooked lobsters, producing a
cloud of moisture that wafted out over the lake.

"Look," I said, pointing north. An undulating curtain
of greenish light shifted across the stars of the Big Dipper,
slowly encompassing the entire northern horizon.

"How considerate," said Harold, "for an aurora to show up at the sauna."

I mentioned the geomagnetic north pole, and our good fortune of being nearer to it than folks in the Eastern Hemisphere, and thus being able to see more auroral displays. We watched the celestial blazonry until satisfactorily chilled.

Back inside, Harold laid some wet cedar boughs on the rocks and in a moment we could smell summer—all soft and green and pungent. The enfleurage of cedar oils was another teasing reminder of spring. Appropriately, the boiler was gurgling and bubbling like breakup itself, and Harold was pleased by the thought that he'd enjoy a supply of warm water for several days. With no electricity or indoor plumbing on the island, it's a fine winter luxury.

A quarter hour later Harold and I returned to the outdoor bench to watch the aurora. It had settled down to a slightly pulsating glow, an accent for starlight and snowfields.

"Oh, by the way," said Harold, "did you hear the news?"

"About what?"

He told me that Jeff, a mutual acquaintance, had died of cancer that very day. He was forty-two. I was shocked; I hadn't even known he was ill. True, I hadn't seen or talked to Jeff for a couple of years, but he'd been a childhood playmate, only a year older than me. I suddenly recalled that I once traded him two toads for a garter snake a very long time ago. Because he was slightly retarded, Jeff had endured occasional cruelty from other kids and was never really our friend in the usual sense. He'd been a curiosity, was even feared a little, and though he had functioned well enough in adult life it seemed particularly sad and unfair that he should die so young from a terrible disease. I really had no idea how he had viewed life, but at that moment I felt bitter in his stead. Statistically, at least, he should have lived another thirty years in sunlight and moonlight before he was slipped beneath the surface of the planet.

"Man, that's too bad," I said. "I'm sorry to hear it." And I was. But the aurora was still stunning and the sauna still hot. Tapping the remarkable capacity we have for sorting and labeling, I shifted my mental image of Jeff from the file of the living to the file of the dead. We often forget or, more accurately, mis-remember things about people—their names, ages, addresses, occupations—but unless we're ill or very old, once made aware we seldom forget who's gone. We often dial wrong numbers, but we don't even try to telephone the dead.

As I toweled and dressed, I savored the aura of well-being and deep cleanliness that a sauna engenders, but I was also subdued. Harold keeps some antiques in the anteroom of the sauna and one is an old metal sign for Climax Plug Tobacco—The Grand Old Chew. I'm an on-and-off user of Copenhagen snuff, and several years ago I was suddenly horrified by the thought of mouth cancer—so much so that I quit cold turkey and was tobacco-free for eight months. I gradually backslid into moderate use with periods of abstention, and occasionally I still worry about cancer. And now, here was Jeff, dead at forty-two, and though not a snuff user so far as I knew, had attained a climax nevertheless. I was irritated to even think of it; my well-deserved sauna buzz was in danger of ruin. It was no time to contemplate mortality—on the eve of March 1, three weeks shy of the vernal equinox.

In single file we headed up the hill toward Harold's log cabin, damp hair stiffening in the cold. Through the canopy of large pines was an island of open sky. Perfectly centered, and fringed by frosted needles and boughs, I could see Orion. Viewed in such isolation the seven most prominent stars appeared much brighter than normal, and their names, memorized in childhood, abruptly surfaced as if written in the sky: Betelgeuse glowing red in Orion's right arm; Bellatrix, dimmer and in his left arm; Rigel, bluish and down at his feet; Saiph, the other foot; and then the three stars of his belt: Alnitak, Alnilam, Mintaka. I stared, trusting my feet to keep the familiar path.

Jeff was dead. But memory was surprisingly stubborn, and his name resisted filing. A stark image arrived unbidden and I saw Jeff in a metal coffin, buried at the frostline in cold and utter blackness. I shivered—partly freezing hair, mostly brittle angst. I consciously battled a surge of dread with the vision of Orion before me. Refreshed by the sauna and hints of spring, and seeing the constellation framed just so by large old pines, I was sure these stars had never been so splendid. Betelgeuse, Bellatrix, Rigel, Saiph, Alnitak, Alnilam, Mintaka. It was poetry inscribed in the heavens, and what kind of creatures could name the stars if the end of their lives consigns them to be forever underground? Perhaps, despite the power of names—Rigel, Jeff—it does; but in the gleam of Orion and the shadows of trees on snow, I could not believe it. The image of the grave dissolved, and as quick as light itself I was buoyant with anticipation.

Inside, Harold's log walls were warm with the orange glow of the fireplace. A pot of aromatic chili simmered on the stove, and as I entered the cozy kitchen my eye caught the glint of glasses, soon to be filled with dandelion wine. I nestled into a comfy old sofa in front of the fire and sighed like a happy dog.

This then, is the chief value of the dead to the living— a vivid joy of contrast. And out of that a vivid wish for rebirth.

17

THE SAME CROOKED WORM

At certain times and places on the trek through space-time, our existence as living organisms on a frequently difficult planet seems wretched. Early passings such as Jeff's, when viewed in the abstract (another wondrous talent of the human mind) can be as appealing as fresh air. While most don't end their lives with suicide, it's often the thought that counts, and one of the roles of an artist is to remind us of alternatives. A masterpiece—in whatever medium—leads us to the edge of life before steering us away from the precipice and back, figuratively, into Harold's sauna on a beautiful starlit evening. Renewal; the caffeine of the soul and the aim of most art, particularly music.

The power of music, from singing wolves to symphonies, lies in the context. For example, we have a quality recording of wolf voices that's interesting to hear (and never fails to wind up The Rev), but doesn't compare to a faint howling just barely heard from the depths of the forest across the lake. Similarly, our relatively cheap CD player simulates the effect of live guitar music to a degree that condemns my first inexpensive record player (mid-1960s) to the realm of the gramophone. But even the best recorded sound isn't in the same league as almost any real guitar picker in a smoky bar on a Saturday night. And if the performer happens to be very good, he or she can lead you to the edge and back.

We were sitting in an Iron Range bar on a cold February night, listening to the kind of performance that made you stare into your beer and be mournful. The guy could sing, and man, could he pick the guitar. Via the texture of his voice and melodies, we were transported—gazing down long empty highways slicked with rain, and listening to distant train whistles in the moonlight. Some of the songs were his own and evoked open roads and bittersweet wanderings.

This middle-aged troubadour was from the Twin Cities, but we'd heard him before. The previous July we'd dropped into a restaurant on Lake Vermilion, and he was there—a one-man band catching the summer resort action. It was late and he was taking requests. The patrons yelled out their favorites—Willie Nelson, Judy Collins, Elvis—he knew them all. And he sang them right. Half the crowd was drunk and heedless, but the man sang as if they were all rapt; as if each moment were important. The owner of the establishment was getting his money's worth. He wasn't doling out his low wage to some honky-tonk tune butcher; he'd hired himself a *minstrel.*

So when we heard this balladeer was going to be playing at a bar in Hibbing, we gladly drove into town. It sounded like a fit palliative for a touch of the dark, deep winter blues. There's nothing like live music and a live crowd inside a warm tavern to inspire hope. Perhaps the sun isn't expiring; maybe April will arrive after all.

Or perhaps not. Although it was Saturday night, there were only two other customers. One was soused, the other was leaving. Our group of three felt smothered by the disheartening loneliness of an empty bar. The distances from vacant table to vacant table seemed long and desolate, like the freezing reaches between planets. Surely a song couldn't survive in this vacuum; surely the singer would wither.

But he was alive, astride a stool on a tiny stage. A single overhead fixture lit the dingy corner. He'd just finished a break, and in a moment his music filled all the dark spaces in the tavern. But he wasn't soothing us, this marantic audience of four winter souls (and one bored bartender). He used his talent to pressure us, to push us up against the world, to make it too much with us. He sang of lost love and forlorn separation, of vanished buffalo and fallen heroes, of icy rivers laced with fool's gold. The lyrics were brimming with disconsolation, but his rich baritone shaped the sadness into phonics of bitter joy. He caressed his guitar into wailing, but it wailed perfectly. He performed with authority, fervent and sincere, as if playing a duet with the Muse. What the hell was this artist doing in saloons?

At his next break he joined us at our table and I bought him a drink. We heaped our praise and he was gracious, but his homesickness and discouragement were evident. He was singing what he felt. We pried, and he told his story. Back in the early sixties he'd had a folk group. It was the golden age of the Kingston Trio, the Brothers Four, and Peter, Paul, and Mary. His group cut a successful folk record in Minneapolis, and in 1964 they seemed to be on their way—they'd been invited out East. He paused and offered us a rueful smile. "We arrived in New York the same week the Beatles did." That was also in

February. The rest was history. He'd played a lot of taverns since then.

We stayed until closing, until long after the lone drunk had stumbled out. We quietly listened to the songs, even more empathetic with the melodious undercurrents of despair. He took our requests and we hummed along, joining in the dirges for dreams. I asked for an old folk song called "Bloody Well Dead." He smiled sardonically and said, "I can't play that; it's too depressing." But he did: "And always remember, the longer you live the sooner you bloody well die."

A half hour past midnight he laid down his guitar. Speaking softly, he noted that Hibbing was the boyhood home of Bob Dylan, and it would perhaps be fitting if his last number of the evening celebrated that fact. I expected a nostalgic 1960s protest song, but he didn't pick up his guitar. Instead he launched into a dramatic recitation of a poem by Dylan Thomas, Bob's supposed namesake. It was a piece he obviously knew well, and the words cascaded off his tongue, acidly echoing through the hollow tavern—conjuring up Dylan Thomas himself, a gifted man with a tragic, untimely end. The last lines, delivered in hoarse ferocity, were:

> The lips of time leech to the fountain head;
> Love drips and gathers, but the fallen blood
> Shall calm her sores.
> And I am dumb to tell a weather's wind
> How time has ticked a heaven round the stars.
>
> And I am dumb to tell the lover's tomb
> How at my sheet goes the same crooked worm.

The minstrel switched off the stage light and walked out the door. It was magnificent. We loudly applauded the empty stage, joyous in our sadness and lifted like eagles by the contemplation of the grave.

18

FIRST ICE

S uch moments of artistic sublimity are rare, and usually whatever happiness and enlightenment we enjoy must be gleaned from the everyday world. It's axiomatic that the more delight we can find in the common, the livelier we're bound to be. In northern Minnesota there's nothing more common than ice, with the exception of mosquitoes, and I've encountered little happiness in the realm of the skeeters.

But ice! Now there's a medium for gladness, particularly the ice of early winter. As Thoreau wrote, "The first ice is especially interesting and perfect, being hard, dark, and transparent."

A couple of Novembers ago we skated on Mark Lake, and we'd never seen such hard ice. Unless your skates were freshly honed, it was impossible to stand up. The blades needed to bite. There was none of the sloppiness allowed by soft, pampered arena ice, where even dull skates can make an impression.

The lake was a sheet of diamond. During a still night near Thanksgiving, a polar air mass had crept down from Manitoba and settled in to change the world. The limpid, mirrorlike surface of the lake had in fact become one. The reflected images of stars were slowly encased in crystal, and by dawn the winter constellations were glinting off a one-inch mantle of ice.

The weather held clear and cold, and two days later we were tentatively exploring the integrity of the sheet. We started at the shore with a cordless electric drill, boring a series of test holes farther and farther out until we were satisfied there were three inches of solid ice out to the middle.

A lake that freezes on a calm night is deceptive. The ice is as transparent as a window, with few bubbles, and it's difficult to determine the thickness by just looking. If there's a crack, it usually extends from top to bottom, and you can study the seam to make a guess. But refraction and depth perception are tricky; we depend on the drill.

Even so, that first sweeping glide away from the land is like a stolen kiss, or the ascent up a tall, shaky ladder—it transmits a fluttering charge down the spine and out to the fingertips. It's an act of faith that you can walk on water. Most skaters start out slowly, involuntarily hunching up their shoulders to make themselves "lighter." But in a few moments the fear vaporizes in a rapidly building sensation of flight. For on clear ice there's a world beneath your skates. There are hills, valleys, and "forests" of aquatic plants. Over shallow water the lake bottom races by, as vivid as a crisp color photo pressed under glass. There are no waves to scatter sunlight and swirl sediment into clouds. On Mark Lake I imagined I was surveying an alien planet, zooming above the "atmosphere" of ice. I could see the submarine world as plainly as if I were in it, but instead I was soaring through my own open space, out in the freedom of blue air.

Soon we were whooping and shouting, pumping along the shoreline, cutting in and out of the little coves, and skirting the frosty trunks of half-sunken deadfalls. Three months before we'd drifted quietly beside these logs in a canoe, casting for largemouth bass, but now all was speed and sailing.

We were intoxicated—overcome by the joy of pure motion. It was as if the governments of friction and gravity had fallen with the temperature. How little effort it required to whip down the lake. It must be how an osprey feels when it catches a thermal over open water and floats on swells of air. We were as free as you can get in two dimensions, unbridled on our flat and vitreous reflection of the sky.

At the east end of the lake, in a shallow nook that's cozy for bass and frogs, there was a wide mosaic of green lily pads, frozen into the ice. It was a splendid still life— last August's flora cast in icy Plexiglas. As I flew over, a movement caught my eye and I skidded to a halt in a shower of crystalline dust. Something was squirming under the ice. I dropped to hands and knees and peered through. It was a huge water beetle, crawling along the bottom of the sheet. Its body was about four inches long and almost two inches wide, and the black spindly legs seemed out of place underwater. It was upside down, belly toward the surface, and as I slid forward, following, we were "face to face." I knocked on the ice with my fist, but there was no reaction—no stopping, no change of pace. We were on opposite sides of a thin but profound barrier—in separate universes. I was only three inches away, but the beetle had no inkling of my existence. I was like an omniscient but impotent god, able to survey the cosmos but unable to enter it.

Although I certainly have in the past. Due to poor judgment I've broken through thin ice on two occasions. I was lucky. It was deep water both times, but also close to shore, and I was able to thrash and flounder through weak ice and slither onto land. I was impressed by (a) how the cold feels like a sledgehammer blow to the thorax and (b) how awkward my breaststroke was while wearing hockey skates and long johns.

Therefore, at least on this first foray of the season, we all wear life jackets and keep a long coil of rope on the shore. Breaking through is embarrassing enough; not getting out alive would be shameful.

But Mark Lake is locked up for the winter, the ice tempered and polished like some strange, gleaming alloy. We're exhilarated and rich—owning fifteen acres of smooth ice. Darting away from the shoreline, we rip out across the lake, digging hard and swinging our arms like speed skaters. We run out of energy before running out of ice, and then rock back and just glide, or twirl into figure eights and yell at the sky. One winter a friend fabricated a sail out of a square sheet of polyethylene. He tied two corners to his ankles, the other two to a broom handle, then held it out front like a fore-royal, letting a brisk northwest breeze scoot him across Little Sturgeon Lake at bicycle speed.

But better than mere velocity is the richness of expanse. That same winter we circumnavigated Big Sturgeon Lake, traversing six or seven miles of ice so smooth and clear that when the lighting was right we skated in harmony with our reflections. I saw my companions in identical pairs—one above, one "below." We darted along the shore, flushing northern pike out of the shallows, deliciously startled by their quick dashes beneath our blades. We twirled and wheeled, reinless mavericks, as privileged as wind. Laughing with exuberence we'd "run" and pump across the wide mouth of a bay until we could accelerate no further, then flop onto the ice, sliding and spinning out of control for fifty yards or more. It was undiluted play, as refreshing as new life.

One glittering night we built a bonfire out on the lake and orbited it like a family of planets in the dark of outer space. The starscape overhead was partially mirrored in the ice, and stars glowed at our feet. I would skate far out into the "galaxy," until the bonfire was an orange speck, then rush back in like a comet from the Oort Cloud, buzzing the flames and digging in for a dizzying turn, leaving a tight parabola scratched in the ice. Where else could I pretend to be a heavenly body?

One reason natural-ice skating is so joyful is that you can't do it every year, and when conditions are perfect you must go for it no matter what—abandoning all obligations to be set free by the ice, childlike, how you used to be all the time, and it's authentic rejuvenation to briefly feel that again. Flashing skates on a frozen lake are a tonic that restores youth.

But soon the snows arrive to end the fling. A transitory nature, of course, is what makes it so precious. That, and the knowledge of what it's like to dance on water.

Play is only one facet of the ice sheet. It's also a
renewable resource that can be harvested like
timber—with chain saws. The first time I "made
ice" it was the third week in January, and the temperature was zero degrees Fahrenheit.

"It's a perfect day for making ice," said Dugan, sniffing
the air. "Not too cold, not too warm."

Dugan and his family need a lot of ice. Their cabin is
on an island, and nothing comes easily except solitude.
There's no electricity available to power the basic appli-
ances that even most rural folks take for granted. And in
blistering July, when the roof shingles turn soft, and
you're slimy in the shade, a cold beer or a tall glass of iced
tea are near to necessities; not to mention the preservation of meat, eggs, and Häagen-Dazs.

They used to haul store-bought ice out to the island all
summer, and Dugan figures they dropped five bucks
every weekend—for frozen water. But why put up with
that expense and hassle when the lake itself is a vast ice
field for five and a half months of the year? The logic is
unassailable. Isn't it smarter to simply harvest and store
the "free" natural ice until you need it? In winter, the
island is literally surrounded by potential ice cubes.

The old-timers gathered ice every year and it was a
thriving industry from Maine to Minnesota. Until a few
decades ago, commercial ice "makers" spent the winters

sawing northern lakes and rivers into marketable chunks and passed the summer vending it in the sweltering towns. The beauty of the scheme was that natural ice is quickly regenerated, a perennial "crop" that requires no cultivation, fertilization, or encouragement of any kind. (And Dugan didn't need a license, a lease, or a permit to go after it.)

Ron, Dugan's son-in-law, knows an old-timer who used to cut and sell ice for a living. Back in the 1930s and early 1940s his friend Henry harvested ice off a lake near Osseo, Minnesota. Once per winter he'd hire about a dozen men for one to two weeks. He had a motorized circular saw mounted on skids that would slide across the ice and could be adjusted for depth of cut. In a commercial operation bulk was important, and they cut large four-hundred-pound blocks. That meant less (though more arduous) handling, and such massive blocks were more resistant to meltdown. Henry's big customers were the taverns, and he stored his ice under a thick blanket of sawdust in warehouses with no roofs. The evaporation of rainfall and other moisture would help keep the ice cool. By all accounts it was a profitable business.

A rough calculation demonstrates the scale of the economics. Assume you have a five hundred-acre, medium-sized lake (there are thousands of them in Minnesota, Michigan, and Wisconsin), and this lake is mantled with twelve inches of ice. If you could cut the entire sheet into manageable blocks, you'd own approximately 1.3 billion pounds of ice. At today's retail price (about twenty cents per pound) that would be more than $200 million worth.

And in a month the lake would be sealed with another twelve inches of merchandise.

Well, Dugan doesn't need that much, and he estimated that with five of us helpers he could fill his eight-by-eight-by-eight-foot insulated icehouse in half a day. This was the fourth winter for this crew, and I was quickly absorbed into a proven system.

The first step was to clear the snow off the ice. Fourteen inches blanketed the lake, and since there was no slush in that particular spot, it was relatively easy shoveling. We cleared a space about eighteen by thirty-five feet and moved about twenty-eight cubic yards of snow, or five dump truck loads. While three of us did that, the other three gathered tools, scooped the sawdust out of the icehouse, and installed four bottles of brandy and schnapps in a convenient snowbank.

Snow cover is a layer of insulation—it's why there's often a stratum of slush on a frozen lake—and as we bared the ice we could hear it, *feel* it, rumbling and cracking as it was rapidly exposed to fresh cold. It's startling to feel the sheet vibrate beneath your boots. The lake is never static, not even in winter.

When the ice was scraped clean, Dugan laid out a length of rope to serve as a guide for a straight cut, and then fired up his saw. He'd filed down the rakers on the chain to minimize resistance and had dumped out the bar oil. Meltwater would lubricate the chain, and we wouldn't have excess oil fouling the ice or the lake.

In pioneer days the cutting was done with a cumbersome, large-toothed blade that was worked by hand.

Besides requiring slavelike labor, the chief disadvantage of the old ice saw was that you couldn't stab into the ice and cut only partway down to open water. You had to be continuously slicing all the way through the sheet. That allowed water to rise up through the saw kerf, and if it was too cold, the cuts would refreeze nearly as fast as they were made. Dugan discovered this the year they cut blocks at minus twenty degrees. He inadvertently punched through the ice and water flowed to the top and solidified instantly. It was like tangling with superglue.

With a chain saw, you can ease the blade in nose-first, burrow to the desired depth (to within an inch or two of the bottom), and then use a jig to hold the bar there as the ice "dust" flies. But it's still hard work. Hunched over a big saw, crabbing slowly along the ice for thirty feet, dumps wind out of your sails in a hurry. We took turns on the saw, making six parallel cuts, about sixteen inches apart. Then two sawyers worked from the middle toward the ends, crosshatching the lines and creating a large checkerboard pattern. It was twenty-two squares long and five wide, or about six by thirty feet. We wanted the eventual cavity to be narrow so we could easily reach the blocks in the middle. You don't want to swim for them.

The next step was to free the first block. Ron had fabricated an ice chisel with a long handle and a wide heavy-duty blade. Using it like a spear, Ron jammed the blade into the kerfs all around one corner block until the layer of uncut ice was broken, and the block was floating free. Then he shoved it straight down. Its natural buoyancy caused it to pop back up like a cork, and as it cleared the surface Joe snatched it with a pair of ice tongs and dragged it up and out. The tongs are antiques, but still an efficient way to handle ice.

With a hole in the checkerboard we had room to work. Bill sawed completely through the end blocks on either side—two or three rows at a time. The chain flung out a rooster tail of cold water, but by this time it was a balmy ten degrees above zero, and flooded kerfs were no problem. Once we had the five blocks of the first row free, Ron could chisel out an entire row at a time and separate each block with a single blow. With four of us wielding tongs, the blocks piled up quickly.

It was like bobbing for apples. The ice was about twelve inches thick, and we'd cut the blocks about sixteen inches by sixteen inches from the top, and since sixteen inches was close to the maximum spread of the tongs, it was easier to snag a block from the side. You'd shove a block under water on one edge, and when it rocked back up at an angle, you could grab it across its twelve-inch depth and heave it out of the water. How convenient, I thought, that ice floats. Aloud, I recalled that it was this characteristic that led to my initial disillusionment with Hollywood. As we happily fished for blocks I told the crew about it.

Several years before I had seen a movie in which a nuclear submarine was sneaking around under the polar ice cap. Something—perhaps a collision—caused the ice above the sub to fracture. It cascaded down in huge chunks, bouncing off the hull. It took a moment for the audience of adolescents and preteens to realize what was wrong, and then we broke into a chorus of hoots and cat-calls. Sinking ice? Give us a break! I was dismayed. If

Hollywood was so dumb about something as basic as ice (hadn't they ever noticed the ice cubes floating in their highballs?), then what other falsehoods were being propagated on film? What pernicious misinformation were we getting about submarines, for instance? I grew as skeptical as Siskel and Ebert.

Speaking of submarines, it would have been a cinch for one of our ice-gathering crew to take a dive. The blocks—which Dugan vowed to cut smaller the next year—weighed about one hundred pounds, and all the splashing caused by our "tonging" had formed a puddle on the surface of the ice. Nothing's more slippery than wet ice. Actually, that's how skate blades work. The pressure of keen edges generates heat to melt the ice and provide a tiny reservoir of slickness.

Such precarious footing made it seem as if the blocks were fighting back. If you failed to yank the ice completely out on the first heave, it pulled you back toward the growing chasm. Wrestling with a hundred-pound block at the very rim of open water seven feet deep required concentration and good form (and unworn boot tread), and I decided I'd wait until that phase of the operation was done before I sampled the brandy.

The blocks were clear when they emerged from the lake—like cubes of cut glass or giant quartz crystals. But soon after exposure to the cold air they'd begin to turn blue. In a few minutes they were an ethereal shade of translucent turquoise. They cried out for sculpting, but their eventual aesthetic appeal would no doubt reach its apex in a cooler full of beer and pop on an August afternoon.

A twenty-foot wooden chute extended from the lakeshore to the door of the icehouse, and Joe, Matt, and I hoisted the blocks onto the lip of the chute and gave them a shove. Bill and Ron (Dugan had repaired to the cabin to see about dinner—a critical role) snatched them off the chute and simply stacked them in the house. Every few rows they heaped snow onto the blocks and made sure it sifted into every space between. When the house was full, we shoveled the sawdust all around and over the top of the blocks and shut the door. It wouldn't be touched until May.

In three hours, six people had harvested and stored a shade less than five *tons* of hard, clean ice. Dugan mentioned that the previous summer—a long, hot one—the last of the ice had endured until autumn, when they'd cleaned the icehouse and thrown it out. It was a pleasing thought that a touch of winter could linger through the summer and survive full-circle until the lake froze over again. I finally felt free to sip at a brandy bottle, and as I took the first sweet pull, I mused that we couldn't have been much more efficient. And we'd had a good time—laughing, kidding, and nipping at the spirits.

Of course, even in northern Minnesota most ice is now made by machines—automatic freezers that are powered, ultimately, by the burning of a fossil fuel. And nobody has any fun. It's what folks call progress.

I'm no Luddite, and I deeply appreciate my PC (that is, I'm enmeshed in the usual love-hate relationship) and other technological marvels and back-savers of this era, but harvesting lake ice causes me to wonder how far we can safely remove ourselves from "old-fashioned," labor-intensive (even a bit dangerous) enterprises without sacrificing an element of humanness.

Physical struggle emanates from, and feeds back into, the very nucleus of life. Even today, chiefly in the Third World, there are people whose daily routine resembles a particularly nasty boot camp. That's hardly an ideal, and it'll be a happier age when everyone's part of the *First* World. Nevertheless, I'm pleased to hear of recent success stories from prisons that have instituted boot camp-like programs as part of both rehabilitation and "doing time." One reason such tactics can work is that we're automatically rewarded for struggle, both emotionally and biochemically. There's pith to the phrase "It hurts so good." One could spin a convincing tale about natural selection and survival of the fittest to explain our affinity for endorphins, and I've heard speculation that we're evolving to a state where mind will be absolute, and hard-core physical endeavor vestigial. Maybe. But I don't think so.

I might be blinded by the chemistry of my brain, but I believe there's inherent spiritual good in hard labor, that ruggedness is as sublime as wisdom, and is one of its sources. Kahlil Gibran wrote, "You work that you may keep pace with the earth and the soul of the earth. For to be idle is to become a stranger unto the seasons, and to step out of life's procession." It's true you may honestly *work* at a VDT or a desk, but *The Prophet*, through Gibran, was addressing "a ploughman," and it seems to me that even a white-collar knight of the Information Age must somehow manage to partake of physical struggle. It's good, proper, and necessary for humans to sweat, grunt, and occasionally bleed. And it's even better to do it as a team. One of the joys of the ice harvest is the fellowship of the effort, and at least for that time we're no strangers to winter or to "life's procession." No one slipped and fell into the freezing water, but it would have been no tragedy. Although not exactly pleasant, it would have been a most excellent physical struggle, and highly rewarded.

20

CHAIN SAW RHAPSODY

A chief pleasure of work is developing a friendship with tools. As allies in our work—in our lifeblood—well-used tools seem almost animate, and I know people who take the loss or destruction of a tool as hard as the loss of a pet, or even a relative.

When I was a freelance photographer, my trusty old Pentax Spotmatic was as dear as a dog, and cared for all out of proportion to its actual monetary value. Under no circumstances would I loan it out, and when it was hanging around my neck it was as much amulet or talisman as tool.

I now harbor similar feelings for what is probably the most important tool I own—my Stihl 038 chain saw. Understand, I'm a staunch environmentalist, a fanatic, some of my neighbors contend (there's a Greenpeace decal on my hatchback), but I dearly love my chain saw. I'll let friends borrow the car, the computer, will even loan out books, but *nobody* touches my Stihl 038. I'm passionate about what we term wilderness, support its protection wherever wild land can be set aside, and have committed time and effort and treasure to the cause, but . . . Wait; let me share an anecdote.

As smoke jumpers in Idaho's Nez Perce National Forest prepare to parachute to a wildfire, their many tactical decisions include whether or not to use a chain saw. If the fire is burning territory designated "wilderness," then a chain saw may not be dropped without express approval from the proper Forest Service authority. Permission (via radio) will almost certainly be granted, but woe to the smoke jumper squad leader who doesn't ask. Chain saws and wilderness are considered incompatible, and only the emergency of fire and the protocol of official request will get one kicked out the door of a jump plane.

It's not the idea of sawing. If smoke jumpers wish to perform any cutting chores with the old-fashioned two-person crosscut saws they also carry, then permission is not required, and obviously a stump left by a crosscut is still very much a stump.

Chain saws *are* noisy, and engine racket is an irritation in the wilderness, but it's questionable whether a power saw is more offensive than the jump plane itself—usually a loud twin-engine aircraft—that may orbit a remote drop zone at relatively low altitude for thirty minutes or more.

A Forest Service booklet titled *Fire Suppression Standards in Wilderness* emphasizes "light hand tactics" and in all caps commands, "MINIMIZE cutting of trees." Well, anyone who's tried it will likely agree there are few more efficient ways to minimize cutting than making folks do it with handsaws—especially when the sawing involves mature timber. But aside from this backhanded pragmatism, the banning (or at least frowning upon) of chain saws in wilderness is largely symbolic. In the public mind, chain saws are to clear-cuts as guns are to crime. Saws, we figure, are threatening not only the spotted owl and everything that species represents, but also the great rainforests of the planet.

Intellectually, we acknowledge that the saw is merely a tool ("guns don't kill people; people kill people"), but a study recently published in the *Journal of the American Medical Association* strongly suggests that gun-control laws enacted in Washington, D.C., in 1976 have made a difference. Should we also have chain-saw control regulations? Can we afford unlimited access to powerful cutting machines for any moron with a yen to drop trees? We can, for the moment. Unlike squeezing the trigger of an AK-47, operating a chain saw long enough to inflict serious damage usually mandates considerable effort and personal exposure to hazard; some natural weeding out of morons occurs. But if society ever sees fit to keep chain saws from the irresponsible, then education in the nature of saws and trees will be critical, and my own chain saw schooling might perhaps be the ideal: it was long and hard. If permits are ever necessary for packing a chain saw, I'll have one. Bronzed.

In June 1973, a logging contractor in the Cascades— "The Hook," as he was called—handed me a chain saw. It was a McCulloch SuperPro 81 with a thirty-inch bar, the first power saw I'd ever hefted. It was a no-nonsense, big-league, can't-find-it-in-the-Sears-catalog production machine, designed for felling the old-growth Douglas fir that was making us all rich—at least by blue-collar standards. (In ten hard weeks on that logging crew I saved enough money to buy a decent used pickup and pay for half my senior year at a private college.) The Hook offered me five minutes of instruction in a matter-of-fact tone suggesting that any American male my age (twenty-two) was surely familiar with a manly tool like a chain saw, and I probably required only a brief review of the fine points of this particular model. I was both flattered and frightened.

Having grown up in northeast Minnesota, where logging is, if not king, then at least a prince, I had long associated chain-saw skills with manhood. Truth was, though, I had been denied that specific rite of passage, and the SuperPro 81 looked terribly potent. But in the humbling presence of The Hook I swallowed my fear and just listened intently. Fortunately, no one entertained the faintest trace of a notion that I'd be permitted to fell 150-foot Douglas fir, and The Hook's minicourse was sufficient to steer me through the now-and-again trimming I had on the landing. And Lord knows, whenever I cradled that big yellow Mac I felt like king of the mountain.

Actually, by the end of summer I understood exactly enough about chain saws to be a menace. The following spring, on the strength of my Oregon experience, I was hired by an East Texas rancher to clear trees for a fence line. He provided the saw. I had been cutting loblolly pine for two or three hours when the saw clattered, snorted, and expired. I noticed the housing was too hot to touch and soon learned that I had fried the clutch and violated the engine. Incredibly, I was ignorant of an axiom: When a chain saw is under load (that is, cutting) there's only one mode of operation—wide open and howling. The meek, in this case, are not blessed, and inherit only shame. "Good job, Mister Big-Time Logger."

The rancher's sarcasm was biting and deserved, and my face was the color of the bright red Homelite I had just trashed. To fail as a sawyer was to fail as a man, or at least as a *yeoman,* that respected species of all-American who's a master of machinery and a self-reliant jack of all trades (and master of some).

Thus, a few years later, when I was preparing to heat a house with wood back in Minnesota, and contemplating enrollment as one of "Mother's Lifers," I decided I'd make firewood the "traditional" way—with a handsaw. I convinced myself it would be safer, quieter, and, borrowing from Ivan Illich, more "convivial." I also convinced a friend he should help me, and we industriously bucked up about a quarter of a cord (I needed six or seven) before concluding that tradition was extinct.

So I purchased my first chain saw. Still intimidated, I selected a small Pioneer with a fourteen-inch bar. It weighed little more than a five-quart pail of ice cream and had about as much guts. "A hedge trimmer!" The Hook would've spat. But I felt less uneasy with it, and pored over the owner's manual before I even touched the recoil. It was fairly comprehensible as manuals go, and via that snippet of formal chain saw learning I gleaned an inkling of how little I really knew.

Over the years I had reluctantly realized that I'm not "structural." One of my boyhood pals could observe a machine, tinker with it, tear it partway down, fondle the pieces, and in a matter of several minutes understand it. By age fifteen he was rebuilding auto engines without an hour of formal mechanic's training. To me, it was wizardry. He'd listen to an engine, poke around under the hood for a minute, and glibly diagnose some carburetor malady. "How do you know this stuff!" I'd demand. He'd shrug. How could I *not* know? Hell, I was reduced to studying manuals, deciphering instructions written by people who didn't need them, and who therefore produced directions as obscure as Mayan glyphs. My frustration would funnel back into ignorance in a vicious vortex of skinned knuckles, stripped threads, and curses.

Even so, the little Pioneer didn't scare me very much, and maybe that's why it inflicted my first chain-saw laceration. The saw was undersized for the performance I was expecting, and also chronically dull, so we both had to work harder. In a moment of carelessness engendered by fatigue on a hot day, I simply ran the saw into my leg, just above the knee. It didn't hurt that badly at first, and I stared at the bloody rip in my jeans, not believing my clumsiness or the treachery of this little saw I'd tended so considerately with top-quality bar oil, the proper fuel mix, and a consistently clean air filter. (The damn machine rode with me in the front seat of the pickup— like a pal—never back in the dirty box!)

Chain-saw wounds are gouged and ragged, filthy trenches in the tissue that require aggressive scrubbing (and probably a tetanus booster) and a lot of stitches. I was lucky to need only five—the single advantage of a small saw. Ultimately, I'd suffer three such humiliating injuries in a five-year span, all caused by overworking myself and weak, dull saws. It's one of those pervasive ironies of life: a sharper, more powerful saw is a safer saw; it lays fewer demands on human and machine, and commands greater respect. I've never left a single drop of blood or shred of skin on a finely honed chain. For years I kept two chains on hand, and as soon as one dulled I'd slap on the replacement and drop the other at a local shop that charged $2.50 to dress it up. It could wax expensive; doesn't take diddly to blunt your saw teeth. A chain whips around the bar at about fifty-five miles per hour, meaning that six hundred cutters per second pass any given point. If you inadvertently stick the roller nose into the dirt (not difficult at all), each cutter can tunnel through sand, clay, or gravel several times before you react. Sparks fly. Dullness. Or you can work too close to the garage, as I once did, and have a kickback ram the saw bar into a concrete footing, destroying not only the chain but also the bar itself—$45 damage in a tenth of a second. (It would have been less embarrassing, and no more costly, to rip another five-stitch gouge in my leg.) Even without screwups it was nothing to wear the edge off both chains in an hour. I often cut trees growing on the margins of dirt roads, and their bark was impregnated with dust; it was like harvesting sandpaper.

The turning point in my relationship with chain saws arrived when I finally learned how to properly employ a round file to hone the cutters myself. It's a simple operation, but many have trouble doing it correctly, and sloppy filing can be worse than none. It's like this: You buy a saw and a file (a filing jig usually comes with the saw), glance at the drawings in the manual, and seeing how easy it is you begin ruining your original chain shortly thereafter; it's never sharp again. Continual discontent leads to an inferiority complex and lots of dollars spent on professional sharpening—not to mention the wasted time and inconvenience of trips to the shop, and additional aggravation when the chain isn't ready when you need it. Add the insidious shame of farming out a simple task that any self-respecting yeoman should be able to handle.

My filing epiphany came during a forest fire in Idaho. Our crew was building miles of fire line—digging, scraping, cutting—and a team of professional fallers was assigned to take out the nastiest snags and perform the lion's share of the sawing. I was packing a government saw, so during a break I watched one of the pros sharpen his chain; I knelt at his feet like an acolyte and he graciously offered me a single tip about how to hold the saw while filing that revolutionized my technique. The secret was in the posture and positioning, and for the first time in my life I could actually *feel* a cutter shedding dullness as I filed. It was exhilarating. Ever since, I've owned only one chain at a time, happily honing away in the field, perhaps seated comfortably on a stump, and never struggling with a dull saw. My annual firewood chores (about eight cords) are more joyous, and I shouldn't require a tetanus booster for some time.

My chain-saw friendship blossomed when we built our log home. All the critical work—sizing, notching, trimming—was lovingly performed with a second Pioneer (a bigger one). I spent long hours roughing out notches while balancing on logs eight or ten feet off the ground, saw screaming and wind grasping at my footing. I fell once, screaming saw in hand, but I held it away from my body and absorbed the impact with my back. We weren't hurt.

In the past few years I've reached a dubious plateau of chain-saw competence. It was partly accidental. On a Minnesota wildfire one of the local foresters happened to see me successfully drop a particularly wicked snag. He wasn't close enough to see the luck involved. A few months later he recommended me to a logger in need of sawyers. I was at an economic nadir, so I hired on for five dollars an hour, falling and limbing mature red and white pine. The Hook would have been proud, but this local logger had no insurance, and I was broke enough to have no brains. If there's a sweatier, more hazardous method of reaping forty dollars a day in a Western nation, it probably involves hammers, boulders, and armed guards. But the logger admired my technique—said so before witnesses—and that covered a multitude of sins. At least at that place and time, by God, I was a *yeoman*.

But the absolute high point was a few months before, at that forest fire in Idaho. The saw was a government-issue Homelite—bright red and quite similar to the hapless unit I'd abused in East Texas fifteen years before. My filing was now in sync, my confidence high, and our crew was in the big middle of the battle. One afternoon I was directed to a huge fir. It was blackened and dead, but 120 feet tall, and still burning. Windblown embers spewed from its top, threatening to ignite spot fires beyond the control line. It had to come down. But the monster was forty-eight inches in diameter, and up till then I'd never felled one that was more than twenty inches. Indeed, my official "Incident Qualification Card" (a firefighter's wallet-sized credential) listed me as a FALB—Faller Class "B." As far as the federal bureaucracy was concerned, I could only drop a tree that was in the "B" range, twenty-four inches or smaller. But there are two sets of rules: pre-fire and fire. When, as Kurt Vonnegut says, "the excrement hits the air conditioning," you just do what needs to be done.

I was intimidated by that fir. It was on the scale of *topography*, and the Homelite sounded tinny in the shadow of its bulk. (I'm aware there are some who say a Homelite *always* sounds tinny.) I studied that tree like a contract, searching for the dendrologic fine print that would determine my tactics. Fortunately it had a slight lean that wasn't exactly counter to what I wanted to do in at least a general way. Thus fortified, I launched into a wide undercut. With my swamper (a sawyer's assistant) keeping an eye out for widow-makers and occasionally gesturing advice over the roar of the saw, I carved out a wedge the size of a coffee table top. The swamper knocked it free with an ax. I executed a dangerous "plunge cut," working the nose of the bar straight in to widen the notch, and then started on the back cut, swinging from one side to the other. Before it was done the twenty-four-inch bar of the saw was buried to the hilt. At the first creaking of heartwood we scurried away like squirrels, neither of us completely trusting my work to tip the trunk in the right direction. When the tremendous burning fir hit the forest floor, the ground shook, raising a mist of ash and soot. The noise of its falling caused firefighters on the opposite flank of the drainage to stop and look around. It lay roughly where I'd intended, and no one was maimed or killed. It was a sweet moment when the swamper slapped me on the back and said, "It wasn't pretty . . . but good enough."

So, after long, difficult courtship I've grown to love my saw. It's a tool of survival: we heat solely with wood. It's a tool of renewal: we own forty acres of trees; I've studied forest ecology, and my judicious cutting promotes optimum conditions for both timber and wildlife. It's a tool of expediency: trees occasionally topple across our driveway. It's a tool for income: I sign on with fire crews (though Lord knows I don't bring my own saw). It's a tool of self-esteem: I'm a semiprofessional sawyer, respected; now I know enough to realize I'm *not* king of the mountain. I'm no longer a menace, and occasionally a yeoman.

However, there is one thing terribly wrong with chain saws, a great mortal sin of their existence, and I admit, I feel a twinge of guilt when I fire up. It's this: in a mere eight hours of operation, a midsize saw like my Stihl 038 will gulp more air than I'll inhale in a lifetime. In the nine years I've owned the 038, it's sucked enough oxygen to service the lives of eleven human beings. In return, it's belched out many cubic feet of noxious exhaust. Despite its grand utility, it's just one more stinking internal combustion engine, filthy and inefficient. It consumes fossil fuel. So far, twenty-five gallons of gasoline and fifteen gallons of bar and engine oil, plus a few tubes of roller nose grease; almost a full barrel of petroleum. In part, the Gulf War was prosecuted in its behalf. When I carry my saw through the autumn woods, its weight is far more than 17.2 pounds. In one way or another, for good and for ill, it bears the responsibility of human life. It both preserves and threatens mine, and that of my family. On the large scale, it both enhances (via the encouragement of tree growth through wise cutting) and degrades the atmosphere of the planet.

I can morally continue to use the saw—prudently, conservatively—only because I understand this. There's a vast difference between mindless use and enlightened use. If I could effectively condense my blood, sweat, and fears, plus a strong dose of forestry and atmospheric science, into a one- or two-hour presentation, maybe it could serve as a mandatory short course for any chain-saw purchaser—both professional and amateur.

We're highly dependent on atmosphere-gulping fossil-fueled machines, and they're not smart; there'll be a better way—has to be. It won't arrive via *my* mechanical skills, but perhaps through some tinkering kid who doesn't read the instructions. When it comes to creating smarter devices, I have faith in the ingenuity of the "structural" ones. For example, there's this from the November 30, 1991, issue of *Science News:* "This fall, the U.S. Office of Naval Research (ONR) spent thousands of dollars trying to encourage university scientists to do what high school senior Christopher P. Stone did with less than $50: blend biology with robotics." The article outlines current studies designed to translate the elegance and efficiency of insects into machinery. Says one computer scientist, "Even the simplest animals are much more versatile than the most sophisticated artificial intelligence machine." This is the brand of open-minded inquiry that may lead to more convivial technology. Who knows? Maybe someday I'll own a hydrogen or solar-powered robotic beaver that'll cut and buck while I stay the hell out of the way where I belong.

In the meantime I'll love my Stihl 038; affection keeps it running right. And hey, let's lighten up on the mere symbols. If the Nez Perce smoke jumpers are going to risk life and limb to fight a wilderness fire (and maybe such blazes should just be allowed to burn—there's a case for it), then cut the red tape and don't worry about the damn chain saws. A stump by any other means is still a stump.

21

COLD COMFORT

The answer is: rhubarb. I'll ask the question later. First, consider corn. An old Penobscot myth reveals that corn was derived from the corpse of the First Mother, who, when starvation threatened the people, had herself slain by her husband and dragged across a field by her sons "until all my flesh has been torn from my body." According to *American Indian Myths and Legends*, this gruesome process seeded the first corn crop: "And they partook of First Mother's flesh and found it sweet beyond words. Following her instructions, they did not eat all, but put many kernels back into the earth. In this way her flesh and spirit renewed themselves . . . generation after generation." It was *production*, the birth of personal agriculture for personal survival.

I suspect there are relatively few in the First World who understand the potency and anxiety of subsistence farming. Imagine the cold bitterness of the fear that would settle in your gut as you watched a storm, freeze, infestation, or drought destroy your crops and those of your neighbors. Just beyond the death of these fragile plants you'd catch a glimpse of your own. It's appropriately disturbing that human gore plays a major role in this myth of the corn. Working the land has often been "a tough row to hoe."

It's a measure of civilization's march that those few who still maintain a tight relationship to the soil are mostly either heavy equipment operators (professional farmers), or gardening hobbyists. The farmers are industrialists and technicians employing a range of machinery, chemicals, and data that place them nearer USX than the Corn Mother, and when I till my own humble soil, I don't consider them brethren—it's nothing hostile, we simply don't have much in common except the dirt itself. And their dirt is different.

The emphasis in personal agriculture—modern gardening—is usually not production per se. It's true that abundance is still sought. For many, however, the chief goal is not a full pantry, but a full soul. Gardening is therapy, a quest for peace of mind. As Joni Mitchell wrote of Woodstock, "We are stardust, / We are golden, / And we've got to get ourselves / Back to the garden." She was, of course, referring to the Garden of Eden.

People still take pride in raising perfect plants, but not because their best hybrid Beef Eater VFN tomato weighed over two pounds, or because their Belgian begonias took "Best of Show," but because a good garden is a demonstration of sincerity, a token of enlightenment. It proves the gardener is intimate with the soil, near to the *roots*—both tubers and human tradition.

Paradoxically, as demonstrated by the First Mother, the essence of good gardening was, and still is, hardship. Perhaps that's the appeal—overcoming. Charles Warner, a collaborator of Mark Twain, wrote, "What a man needs in gardening is a cast-iron back, with a hinge in it." And that's the least of it. Besides the treachery of their own bodies, gardeners face a host of external enemies: insects, disease, rodents, hail, drought, family pets, wind, scav-

enging birds, and what is for me the toughest adversary of
all—cold.

We till the soil at forty-seven degrees, forty minutes
north latitude. I find it ironically amusing that if we lived
at that latitude in France, we'd be a hundred miles *south*
of Paris, and probably nurturing vineyards. As it is, our
winters endure for a full five months or more. According
to my records, we can expect the first subzero weather by
the third week of November, and we've suffered the last
below-zero readings as late as the first week in April.

In such a climate, *phenology* means a lot. According to
Webster's, phenology is "the study of natural phenomena that recur periodically, and of their relation to climate
and changes of season." For instance, one of the harbin-
gers of spring for many in the Upper Midwest and New
England is the first sighting of a returning robin. That
orange breast and cheery call can certainly raise the spirits of a winter-beaten psyche, but for me a more reliable
phenological parameter is the snow cover over our septic
tank. Since the resident organisms generate heat (in a
microbiological frenzy of feeding and reproduction), the
frost leaves the ground over the tank long before it does
anywhere else.

Sometime in February, we notice a depression in the
snowfield. Down below, at the interface of dead grass and
ice crystals, a meltdown is in progress. There's an entire
ecosystem buried out there, prospering. The very first
sign of spring is when bare ground appears over the septic
tank. This past year it happened on March 4. Oh, sure,
it's always temporary—the snowfall reinforcements
arrived on March 8—but that ephemeral patch of soggy

brown grass tells us that the back of winter is broken. Further dips below zero will be brief, and lack conviction. In a matter of weeks there will be rainfall.

For a gardener, timing is everything. *When* you do things is usually far more important than how you do them. If we put out our tomato plants or marigolds too early, it matters not how gently we handled the roots, or how well we provided nourishment. Frost is the great equalizer. So our primary tactic in the battle against cold is simply avoiding it.

First, we ignore the planting recommendations on the backs of seed packages, in seed catalogs, and in gardening books and almanacs. Except in very broad terms, those zones and maps depicting climatic regions and "when to plant" are useless. No matter where you live, there are local variables that can be critical. One year, our last frost was on June 16, and our first "autumn" frost was on August 11. That was a freak summer, but with only one exception in the past thirteen years, we've had one or more killing frosts in June, and nearly as many by the end of August—every season. You won't find that data reflected on a chart of planting zones—unless it's a map of the Northwest Territories.

You must develop your own guidelines, and there are two sources of reliable information: personal records, and the advice of local gardening veterans. I maintain a phenology calendar on which I record frosts and *near*-frosts every year, starting on May 1 and going to September 30. Since our thermometer is about thirty feet from the garden, my data is indeed local—and it needs to be. We have neighbors who live only a mile away, and they enjoy a growing season that's usually three weeks longer than ours. Their gardens are near a lake, and the body of water acts as a massive heat sink, moderating the temperatures around its shore.

Gardening is an art as well as a science, and the experience and theories of old hands are an invaluable source of guidance. If someone's been hassling with the vagaries of neighborhood weather for thirty or forty years, chances are she'll have a firm handle on *when* to do things. I've talked to people like this. Rare is the expert who isn't delighted to rattle on about what he or she knows—in detail.

One of our neighbors, who's been gardening for most of her eighty years, never puts out a tomato plant before June 10. Until then they're safely ensconced in a cold frame. Using that date as a base, and considering that her garden is near a lake, I've studied my own records and determined that we should never put out a tomato plant until June 12. Nine out of ten years we'll be safe.

But there's always the potential for a wild card, for the maverick high-pressure ridge out of Manitoba in mid-June (or mid-August). When you can't out-maneuver the cold, you're forced to confront it. The main weapons in our arsenal are an alarm clock and a garden hose.

Other than a nightmare, the only thing that will rouse me an hour before dawn is our obnoxious electric alarm clock. Once awake, what actually forces me out of a warm bed is the vivid memory of the previous evening's weather forecast; and I don't wait for an official meteorologist's frost warning. It's usually not local enough. I note the predicted low. If the weather report on KAXE radio forecasts a low of thirty-eight to forty, our garden will almost certainly be frosted. A 90 percent chance, to use the meteorological parlance. If it's below forty degrees, I set the hateful alarm so I can check our thermometer before sunrise. If the reading is thirty-five degrees or lower, I stumble out into the murky predawn and grope for the garden hose. In springtime, Arcturus, Regulus, and a few other bright stars are still visible as I shower tender young plants with life-preserving mist. Water is warmer than ice. The tomatoes, peppers, and other sensitive plants may be shocked and offended, but they'll survive.

We live in a cold spot. Few of our neighbors have frosts as late or as early as we do. One of our neighbors whose garden is near the lake is guaranteed about a full additional month of frost-free days. Still, there are others, far from water, who aren't nipped nearly as often as we are. For years I wondered why. What made our garden one of the preferred targets of old Jack Frost?

I learned the answer from *Harrowsmith*, a Canadian gardening and rural lifestyle magazine. We find it helpful to take advice from folks who grow tomatoes *north* of us. I was absolutely inspired when I read of a gardener in the Yukon, happily composting at sixty-five degrees north latitude and planting over *perma*frost. Our garden site is tropical by comparison. Still, according to the frost experts there are two important factors going against it. First, it's an isolated opening in the forest. All around us the woods stretch out, dense and relatively unbroken; in some directions for miles. Cold air will flow along the treetops and, like water, drop into any depression it finds. Our yard is a hole in the forest, a trap for the heavier cool air. Second, our woodland clearing is also at the top of a rise. The Canadians assured us that the coldest parts of a slope are the base and the summit. Ideally, a garden plot should be in the "thermal belt" at the middle.

So now I know; it's comforting. When I'm out there on dim early mornings groggily brandishing the hose and jousting with June frosts, I understand why it's happening, and that makes the battle a little easier. Know your enemy. That's what the late-spring frost is: the final assault of sick old winter. The harsh antagonist has been around too long once again, and before he's recycled completely by fiery July, there's nothing he'd like better than to drag our sweet corn and tomatoes down with him.

If it's convenient—that is, if the plants are still relatively small—I'll sometimes cover them the evening before, especially if the meteorologists are screaming about a *killing* frost. That usually means that *our* garden will suffer an onslaught of temps in the low twenties. My preferred covering materials are cardboard and egg cartons. I cut the cardboard boxes into panels that I can simply fold into tentlike structures. The egg cartons, of course, are prehinged, and many are now made of some kind of rigid foam that is an excellent insulator. They're very light, but since frosty mornings are invariably *still* mornings, that's not a problem.

In addition to avoiding cold or fighting it, you can also enlist allies against cold. These are plants themselves, certain kinds and varieties that can endure, and sometimes even thrive, at low temperatures. I'm not holding my breath until the arrival of the frost-resistant bell pepper or dahlia, but there are several plants tough enough for northern springs and autumns. Root crops such as carrots, beets, and parsnips will not only survive a frost, but properly mulched they can be harvested fresh all winter. Asparagus doesn't mind a chilly May, and our Sugar Ann and Sugar Snap peas do well in cooler weather. Members of the *Brassica* genus, such as cabbage, broccoli, and Brussels sprouts, actually love cold weather, and our broccoli looks positively anemic until blessed by the bracing mornings after Labor Day. We also plant the varieties of sensitive crops that are speedy growers. For example, we love sweet corn, but the season passes in a flash, so we work only with Earliking, a hybrid that matures in sixty-six days—significantly sooner than "normal" corn.

Among the flowers, we've seen our tulips bravely bearing up under two inches of April snow—a truly bittersweet sight. The crocuses are determined to push out of the newly thawed soil and bloom long before it's good for them.

Despite these heroics, the easiest way to nurture plants in the north would be to have your own greenhouse—a big one. But we compromise. Early on, I built a cold frame (or hot box, as some call it). It's a three-by-six-foot wooden box with two-foot sides, painted black inside and out to absorb more solar heat. Three old storm windows serve as greenhouse glass, and even when the temperature is below freezing, it's toasty inside the frame. After sensitive plants such as peppers, tomatoes, and most flowers get too big for the kitchen windowsill, they can be stored (and encouraged) inside the frame until it's safe for them to be out in the garden proper.

Nevertheless, it's a trial. Cold is powerful and our personal victories are small, always defensive in character. Jack Frost has us by the throat, and we just manage to escape—never the other way around. Except in one case; and then it's not the gardener, but the vegetable (or fruit?) itself. What common garden plant, requiring *no* human attention so far as I can determine, and multiplying like a virus, is so impervious to cold that every spring we see it thrusting up through *frozen* ground and snow cover, surviving even subzero temperatures? That's the question. Unfortunately, as indicated, the answer is rhubarb.

This rough-and-tumble bully of a plant, with its sour, stringy fruit and poisonous leaves, will annex your entire garden if you let it. Except for biomass, and the occasional sauce or pastry, rhubarb's value is chiefly aesthetic—something green and red and thriving when all else is still intimidated by the rearguard of winter. Why aren't corn or cantaloupes so hardy and belligerent?

Well, if through some cultural quirk rhubarb should become a staple, as popular as, say, sugar or tobacco, I shall forsake all other pursuits and plant ten acres of it. Then I'll sit back and laugh at the cold until the rhubarb has made me rich. Dream on, dream on; the First Mother showed us there's no such thing as a free lunch.

But even when it's cold, our climate isn't always harsh. Consider the first frost of autumn.

It smells blue. That first breath of early-morning, late-August air feels as cold as clear winter sky. It smells clean, like crystals of new November ice, and within that crisp inhalation is the tangy scent of dry leaves and stems. The roof of the cabin is a white tapestry, each shingle limned with frost, traced as if by grand design. Soon this morning freeze will be routine, a daily accent, a seasonal hardening to prepare the land for snow. But this first frost is refreshment. Sultry summer days were welcome once, but now it's time for heat to be gone. Frost is Nature's ice cream, a cool white treat. It's a balm for sunburn and sweaty linen sheets. The tomatoes and corn are done, but they lived a full life, and the marigolds near the house are still OK and will probably endure through half of September.

It's not a vindictive snap. You've had your chance at gardening. The first frost is a harbinger, a sparkling dusting of barely made ice. Change is in the air. That's good; it's time for a change. It's time for the maples to turn crimson and orange, and the aspens to quake all yellow. It's time for cool, dry evenings and turtleneck sweaters. It's time for flushing grouse out of the hazel brush and searching for cranberries down in the bog. Just beyond the rim of yellow-red autumn lies a reborn winter. It's welcome now; skis and long quiet nights, stars brilliant and steady. The first frost is a preview of coming attractions. Perhaps tomorrow we'll have the second frost. Good, it's time. Besides, we may as well spin along with the cycle; Nature will not be dissuaded.

22

T R I C K S T E R   T A L E S

I t's wise to be mindful of the laws of Nature. Duke and Sandy weren't. Of course, Sandy is a golden retriever, and she wasn't driving the truck, so most of the blame lies with Duke. This is how I heard the tale:

The highway was slippery when they pulled out of a congenial roadside nest called the Viking Bar. Duke probably reminded himself to be careful and then forgot. On the way to Togo ("Where the asphalt ends and The North begins") competing traffic is not a problem, and Duke was mesmerized by the lonely sheen of his headlights on the icy roadway.

A few miles west of the Viking, near a narrow bridge that spans Bear River, there's an old gas station that has been converted into a private residence. Normally you'd never want to live that close to the highway, as Duke was soon to demonstrate.

The old gas pumps are long gone, but their concrete island remains, an imposing slab of concrete about six inches high. I suppose Mr. Johnson figured it was easier to just leave it than to take the trouble of busting it up and carting it off, or maybe he thinks of it as a barricade— a buffer between his house and the highway. Whatever the reason, it was a good idea.

As he approached the bridge, Duke lost control of the pickup. It was Nature, the laws of physics. As most Northerners know, you're usually OK on a slick road as long as you maintain a steady course and speed. The steering wheel and brake pedal are on hair triggers. When you alter either direction or velocity, you're courting trouble, and you've got to ease into it. Well, Duke made some sort of abrupt change and spun off the road. The truck skidded into Johnson's driveway and struck the concrete island—broadside. The truck stopped. The passenger door flew open and both occupants were thrown out. Sandy was in the lead. Hunting dogs are like that.

Fortunately, there was a large picture window where the front of the gas station used to be. Sandy went through first. Say what you will about broken glass, but at high velocity it's far better to pass through glass than a solid wall. Duke said later he was grateful that his dog had blazed a trail through the window. He was satisfied that his lacerations would've been much worse if he'd gone through first.

Inside, Mr. Johnson was watching TV when Duke and Sandy arrived. One moment there was the even electronic glow, and the next a sudden draft and noisy reality. His visitors were sprawled in a puddle of glass behind the couch, dazed and bleeding, but not seriously injured. They weren't necessarily unwelcome, but certainly uninvited.

One report has Mr. Johnson saying, "Well hell, Duke! The door was open." But it sounds apocryphal. I suspect he uttered a series of profane exclamations and then either chuckled or growled, depending upon his insurance coverage and his general outlook on life. He was certainly thankful for the concrete island—and the fact that the gas pumps were gone. He was also glad he hadn't been sitting in front of the window. It pays to be mindful of the laws of Nature.

Sandy reminds me of the time our own golden retriever—The Reverend's predecessor—was missing for twelve days. Jim was eleven years old and taking life slow, and it wasn't like him to leave the back porch for very long. He'd lost interest in chasing squirrels and rabbits and was now usually content to study their antics from a prone position. If a dog can be wise, he was. If he had learned to talk, I'd have listened closely and taken notes. Nevertheless, he wandered off on the afternoon before the deer season opener, and though his coat was reddish, it wasn't even close to blaze orange. When he was still gone the next day, we were afraid he was going to get shot.

We meticulously searched the woods within a mile or so of our cabin, calling his name all the while. Once, Pam thought she heard his bark off in the distance, but we found no sign of him. Jim was well liked, and we spread the word among our friends and posted notices at the post office, the store, and a local tavern. We mounted a daily search, but as days passed hope dwindled, and the sight of his forsaken food dish grew ever more poignant. November weather turned bleak, and the first four inches of snow arrived. The woods were becoming inhospitable, and we thought Jim was gone for good.

Then one afternoon I stepped outside and froze in my tracks. There was Jim standing in the driveway—looking far more than half dead. It was instantly obvious what had happened. He'd spent the better part of two weeks trapped in somebody's snare. The hair and skin around his neck were gone. From the base of his ears to his shoulder blades, the snare wire had excoriated him down to raw muscle tissue. The six-inch collar of horror was caked with dried blood, and fresh fluid was dripping into the snow.

My heart sank and tears welled up. Nature said this dog should be dead, and my first sickening thought was that I'd have to shoot him. I called his name and ran to his side, and was amazed when his lips parted in a "grin" and he wagged his tail. There was some life left. I filled his dish, set it down under his nose, and the tough old hunter began to wolf it down.

All right! If he could wag and wolf, it couldn't be as bad as it looked. I phoned the vet to warn him, then gently hoisted Jim into the cab of our pickup and sped toward town. Within five minutes the stench inside the truck was overpowering. Despite subfreezing temperatures, I rolled the window all the way down and trusted my nose to make the necessary adjustments.

Our vet was a seasoned practitioner, but even he recoiled at the first glimpse of Jim's bared neck. He admitted there wasn't much he could do without administering a full anesthetic, and Jim was too weak for that—he'd probably never wake up. We'd have to build his strength for a couple of days. He said Jim's age had probably saved his life. A younger, more energetic dog would have struggled until the snare strangled him. The snow and cold weather had also been a blessing. Eating snow had spared Jim from total dehydration, and the cooler air had kept the wound free of flies and maggots.

We fed and pampered the old retriever for two days, then returned to the vet. He thoroughly cleaned the wound, sprinkled it with sulfa powder, and that was it. Nature, he said, would do the rest. And oh yes, we might dose it regularly with Adolph's meat tenderizer—it would help to keep it clean.

Pam and I were skeptical, but I'd noted that Jim had seemed unimpressed by the injury himself. Once he'd been reunited with his food dish and his favorite rug, he sank comfortably back into meditation. Since his tongue wasn't long enough to reach around the back of his head, there wasn't much he could do about it anyway.

To our astonishment it required only a week or so for the ripped folds of skin to knit back into a covering for the muscle. There was no trace of an infection. In a month only the hairlessness was a clue to the severity of the wound, and by the first day of spring we had to *search* for scars. A casual observer wouldn't have had the slightest suspicion that Jim had been nearly decapitated.

But there was no need for any of it. By law, a trapper is supposed to check his snares every thirty-six hours. Jim had suffered for twelve days. We don't know who the trapper was, but if I ever find out, I'll . . . well, I hate to tip my hand, but it's a procedure that involves a length of snare wire and some Adolph's meat tenderizer. Nature will take its course.

But then it always does, even when you can't believe it. One of the truly awe-inspiring things I've seen was a simple manifestation of gravity and mechanics, but I doubt it'll happen again in a thousand years.

Many years ago three of my buddies and I were on a wilderness backpack trip. Two of us were sixteen, the other two were fourteen. Being teen-age American males, we were basically idiots, but Milt bore the additional burden of being a nerd. A few years later he was sporting shoulder-length tresses as a member of a rock band, but at age fourteen he was a crew-cut, round-faced do-gooder with eyeglasses that weighed a pound and were perpetually strapped to his head. He was trying hard, but he really had no business on that trip. Besides our cruel teasing, he had to lug his unathletic body through the wilderness. His feet hurt, his legs hurt, he wasn't enjoying himself. The rest of us suffered too, but we kept it to ourselves.

Spinoza said that "nature abhors a vacuum," but Nature also seems to bear a grudge against the vulnerable. On the third morning Milt had diarrhea, encouraged, no doubt, by our trail food. Aside from death through torture (or election-year television) there's nothing worse than a case of the runs in the wild. It starts with the rationing of toilet paper and descends from there. But Milt was to be our Job, and watery intestines were only the beginning.

Since we'd first set out on our seventy-mile trek, Milt had lagged behind. We'd periodically stop and wait for him, but gradually these halts grew more infrequent. By mid-afternoon of day four, it had been several hours since we'd seen him.

"Hey," said John, "we'd better wait for Milt."

"Who?"

"C'mon, let's take a break and give him a chance to catch up."

So we dropped our packs and sat around for nearly an hour. I started to worry. The kid couldn't be *that* far behind. Goaded by guilt, we left our gear and started backtracking in search of our companion.

We'd gone over a mile when I heard a strange noise ahead. It sounded like a puppy with its paw in a rat trap. We rushed around a bend in the trail and found Milt.

I remembered that mudhole. It was a wide spot where moose traffic had churned the trail into a quagmire. I'd gone around it to the right, skirting the mud while pushing a rubbery, low-hanging tree limb out of the way. I'd leaned on the branch to bend it down and away, and then let it snap back when I was past.

Apparently Milt had done the same, but by quirky chance, the limb had snagged the frame of his backpack. When he let it go, the rebounding branch had actually swung him off his feet and out over the mudhole. There he hung, like a hapless jungle victim in a Tarzan movie. He could reach the mud on tiptoe, but not enough to gain a purchase. The straps of the pack had pinioned his arms, and though he struggled, he couldn't free himself. He certainly couldn't reach his canteen (or his toilet paper).

You can imagine the scenario: no one passes that way until the following summer. One day, a horrified Boy Scout stumbles into a skeleton and moldering backpack hanging in a tree. The empty eye sockets peer darkly through a pair of thick glasses.

None of it, of course, was a bit funny to Milt, but we three of his "friends" howled uproariously before we cut him loose. I don't think he ever forgave us, and we probably didn't deserve to be forgiven. I hope, however, that Nature has forgiven whatever grievances she had against *him.*

The Bible says that "time and chance happen to all men," and Milt would no doubt agree, but the vagaries of fortune are not limited to humans. As you know, we keep a bird feeder outside our living-room window, and after a decade of providing this avian dole, we've seen every bird native to the area. We've graduated from merely identifying species to picking out males, females, juveniles, and even individuals (Bob, of course, being the most celebrated).

I was shocked therefore, on a certain mid-November morning, when I glanced out the window and saw an utterly strange bird. I did a double take then pasted my face against the glass. Saying it wasn't a local was an understatement; this bird looked as though it belonged on another continent.

It was about the size of a jay, with a white breast and a brownish back, but its face was incredible. It looked like a Sioux brave in war paint. From just below the beak to the top of its head were a yellow band, a black band, and then another yellow band. Its eyes split the top two bands, with a little black slash curving around to the side. The most notable feature were the two horns sticking out of its head. Horns! I grabbed the binoculars for a closer look. The "horns" were feathers, of course, but the impression was of a Sioux warrior wearing a Viking hel-met.

The bird was pecking tentatively at seeds in the snow—the ones that had been kicked off the feeder by the more aggressive regulars. It looked timid, and it never did actually fly to the feeder. This bird was obviously a transient. I paged through our field guide until I found it. Our visitor was a horned lark. According to the map it was a relatively common species not terribly far to the west and south of us, but it was certainly alien to me. Why was it here? Do birds get lost?

The answer came with the evening news. While the local weathercaster was spouting his customary lies, he mentioned that our recent storm—a violent November blast similar to the one in 1975 that sank the *Edmund Fitzgerald* in Lake Superior—had blown flocks of migrat-ing birds off course and forced them to ground in places they usually avoided. Indeed. The field guide said that in winter the horned lark feeds "in freshly manured fields." Our backwoods yard is more like "bunny berries and bear scat under the trees."

The lark hung around for two days and then was off. It had collected some nourishment, and, we hoped, its wits and bearings as well. But like the road to Togo, Novem-ber skies are slippery and hazardous, and I assumed the bird would need more "time and chance" to make it home.

Nature is fond of curve balls. One September morning I looked out the upstairs window at the sunrise and a strange object caught my eye. It was a shiny lump about the size of a football sitting in the middle of the driveway, with a much smaller dark lump on top of it. I stared and squinted in the dusky light but couldn't decide what I was seeing. Nothing had been there the evening before.

As I headed downstairs and out the door—rousing The Reverend from his rug in the kitchen—I spun playful fantasies about UFO spoor, airliner detritus, and a terrorist bomb. Reality, however, competed with all three.

The shiny object turned out to be The Reverend's steel food bowl, which usually sits at the bottom of the back porch steps about fifty feet from the middle of the driveway. He never moves it. The bowl was upside down, and precisely in the center of the flat bottom was the small dark object—a moist, thumb-sized turd. Rev sniffed it and stiffened, then rushed about the yard in a huff, nose to the ground, hackles high. I laughed, then chided him.

"Ha! See what Mr. Coon thinks of you?"

I had to believe it was raccoon scat, scornfully deposited after the dog food was stolen. Animals do display attitude, and who would be more apt to entertain scorn than an opportunistic, thieving raccoon? (They seem to particularly despise dogs.)

If we may personify Nature—let's flow with the current zeitgeist, name her Gaia, and make her beautiful—then one facet of her personality is a well-honed sense of humor. It's easy to imagine the impish laughter of Gaia resonating in air molecules as poor Milt hung from one of her custom-made whoopee limbs.

Humans admire a finely crafted joke, and our friend Harold is an accomplished practitioner. For example, his telephone used to be on a party line, and Harold has a quick mind. One day he picked up his receiver to make a call and could hear one of the four people who shares his line already dialing. As they finished the final digit, he flattened his voice into officialese and said, "I'm sorry, but you've just dialed an unworking number."

"Oh," replied the caller, and hung up. Harold then made his own call.

Another time, when he said hello in his gruff, pure-blooded Scandinavian manner, there was a brief silence on the line. Then a young woman's voice tentatively asked, "Is this Riverside Sales?"

Harold seized the day. "Yes," he boldly replied. "What can I do for you?"

The woman inquired about renting some cross-country skis. With an air of glib authority Harold informed her of the styles and sizes available, and when they'd settled on waxless skis so many centimeters long matched to such-and-such poles, he politely asked about her time of departure and intended ski route.

"Why do you want to know?" she asked.

"Well," Harold replied, "if you plan to cross Highway 5, I need to know when and where so I can have our crew standing by up there."

"Crew?"

"Yes. They'll shovel snow onto the highway so you can cross in comfort, and also protect the bottoms of our skis. After you pass, they'll shovel it off."

"Oh. How nice."

"Just part of the standard service, ma'am. And oh, by the way, do you have any meatballs?"

"Meatballs?"

"Yes, ma'am. We've had some trouble with timber-wolves lately. Just last week one of our ski poles got chewed up pretty bad. But if you carry some meatballs, you can toss them to the wolves and they'll leave you alone."

"Oh . . . "

"If you don't have any, we can provide a dozen for a nominal extra charge."

"I see . . . well . . . I suppose . . . "

"And oh, there's one more thing, ma'am."

"Yes?"

"You have the wrong number."

It sounds like a nasty thing to do (albeit a benign, W. C. Fields kind of nastiness), but in midwinter allowances must be made. All that second-hand indoor air recycles into your bloodstream and makes you a little crazy; sometimes crazy like a fox.

Native American mythology is replete with trickster tales, and the jokester is often typified by Coyote, or by Iktome the Spider Man (in European stories it was Reynard the Fox). They're rebels and taboo breakers, delighting more well-behaved people with outrageous antics they may secretly admire or envy.

In a tale from the Brulé Sioux, Iktome lusts after a beautiful and naive young virgin, and in an attempt to approach her he dresses as a woman. As they lift their skirts to cross a stream, the virgin notices his penis. She's never seen a man naked, so she doesn't know what it is. Iktome tells her it's a large wart, wished on him by an evil shaman. The girl suggests they cut if off, but Iktome assures her that there's only one way to overcome the evil magic, and that's by placing the wart in her vagina. Wanting to be sisterly, the girl agrees, and sure enough, after this treatment the wart is at least smaller. But not gone. After a second, third, and fourth treatment the ex-virgin tells Iktome that she doesn't think he'll ever get rid of the growth.

"Probably not," he says.

"You may just have to live with it," she says.

"Yes," replies Iktome, resigned, "but let's try once more just to be certain."

The tricksters, though, aren't merely lecherous mischief makers; they also alternate as benefactors, helping the people by cleverly dealing or stealing arrowheads from Obsidian-Old-Man, tobacco from the Sun, fire from the pines, or by outwitting a cheating white trader. Their exploits are ribald and irreverent, and no matter how serious the ostensible topic, the humor has preeminence. In *American Indian Myths and Legends*, a Lakota medicine man named Lame Deer is quoted as saying, "Coyote, Iktome, and all clowns are sacred. They are a necessary part of us. A people who have so much to cry about as Indians do also need their laughter to survive." Gaia seems to understand this.

Authentic clowns are nigh unto priests—mediators between earthy humor and the general pathos of life.

Ronald McDonald, for instance is *not* an authentic clown, merely a puritanical corporate shill. A few of the many recent sanctified clowns are Lenny Bruce, Kilgore Trout, Ford Prefect, and Hunter Thompson before he lost his edge to chemicals.

Sacred clowns are both presenters and interpreters of mysteries. When we're confronted by paradox, or assailed by adversity or absurdity, they make us chuckle and snort after we cry. I don't believe it's accidental that tears are generated by laughter as well as weeping. Gaia puts great stock in water.

The beauty of it is that she may anoint any one of us at any time to be a clown for the sake of our fellows, if only briefly, like Milt. When it's your turn to illuminate a slice of life with some foible, gambit, faux pas, or garden-variety joke, ease in and out gracefully and appreciate your holiness.

It was Montaigne who wrote, "Let us give Nature a chance; she knows her business better than we do."

23

CRY OF THE LOON

I opened this book with stark images of an entity called Windigo and a personal fantasy of dying in the snow with ravens as funeral directors. These images derived from a vision I experienced several years ago on a moonlit winter night. I call it a vision because it wasn't a dream. I was awake and alert and the images simply materialized in my consciousness—forcefully.

This fantasy recently broke into life; not for me, but for a man I never encountered until I saw him dead in the snow.

I'm a member of our local volunteer fire department, a unit that also provides an emergency medical service based on "first responders." They're people trained to administer advanced first aid before an ambulance arrives from town, about fifteen to twenty miles away, depending on exactly where you've suffered your heart attack, car accident, suicide attempt, or other calamity.

I'm a firefighter only, not a certified first responder, and don't rush off to medical emergencies unless firefighters are specifically requested to lend assistance. But via my pager I'm party to all medical calls, and it's interesting and instructive to listen in on the radio traffic, a highly intense form of public broadcasting.

In November 1992, during the Minnesota deer hunting season, the pager announced that a hunter was down in the woods. An ambulance had been dispatched and our first responders were requested at the scene.

When a unit is paged, it's their immediate responsibility to acknowledge the message with a call to the sheriff's department dispatcher, either by phone or radio. There was no acknowledgment by our responders. After the required span of one minute, a second page went out. Nothing.

Yet I was certain we must have a few of our medical people en route. I had just seen some of them out and about less than an hour before, and I guessed they weren't near a phone and didn't have a radio (we don't own as many two-way radios as we sometimes need; they're expensive, and we're not rich). As chief of the fire department, I do have a radio, and I decided I'd better head for the scene to deliver my two-way to the first responders I hoped would be there; they'd need to talk to the inbound ambulance as well as the dispatcher. The page had also mentioned that the victim (of an apparent heart attack) was lying some distance back in the brush, and I anticipated that extra muscle might be needed to portage him out to the road.

It was after dark, and roads were slick with the freezing drizzle that had fallen earlier in the day. My truck fishtailed a little as I exited our driveway onto the main road. It was about eight miles to the incident, and I experienced the acute frustration of the emergency responder who must force himself to drive slowly on the way to a potential life-and-death matter. It's not uncommon in this northern clime, and I've found it effective to actually speak aloud to myself in these situations: "Take it easy, take it easy, don't end up in the ditch—won't do anyone any good."

After several long minutes I pulled off a remote dirt road in front of a hunting shack. I was relieved to recognize two vehicles belonging to first responders; I'd guessed right. Neil had left his headlights aimed down a snow-packed trail behind the shack, and I jogged down it for about a hundred yards.

Four or five hunters were huddled around three of our first responders who were kneeling next to a corpse. He was dead before they arrived. He was lying on his back in the snow, gray-bearded and dressed all in red. I figured he was in his mid-sixties, and he looked almost nonchalant. Aside from a smear of phlegm at his mouth, he could've been napping.

I handed my radio to Janean and she contacted the ambulance with a status report. They'd be able to ease up on the icy highway.

As it turned out, we were able to get a four-wheel-drive pickup almost all the way back to the body, and once the ambulance crew had lashed him to a backboard, six of us hefted the dead weight and carried it a few yards to the tailgate of the truck. We slid the hunter into the box, and the pickup crawled out of the woods.

As Neil and I shuffled through the snow behind the makeshift hearse, I said, "Well, I suppose there's worse ways for an old guy to go."

"Yeah. At least he was out doing something he liked. Didn't die in a hospital bed."

"Really. He could've suffered with cancer or something and lingered for months. He died with his boots on."

Such talk, of course, is meant to comfort ourselves and blunt the stress of the event, but it was also sincere, and I suddenly recalled my vision of ravens and death in the winter. It wasn't quite as poetic out there in the cold glare of flashlights on real snow, but it didn't seem naive either. This hunter had probably experienced some pain as he dropped, and perhaps even panic—if there'd been enough time. (From the evidence, the medical folks assumed he had died quickly.) Even so, it was true; there are many more terrible ways for an old man to quit living than to fall—armed and fully clothed—into the snow of the November forest. The sour aspect was all of us, trampling the trail, digging in the man's pockets for identification, making noise with radios. It all had to be done, naturally; there are simply too many of us in too small a space to leave the dead lying around in the woods, and too many cultural rituals and taboos concerning human death to allow the ravens to play any part.

Janean gave me my radio and I headed home to make dinner. This man had been a stranger, so obviously it was easier for me to deal with his death than it was, say, for his brother, who had watched us load him into the pickup. Still, all in all, I didn't feel I'd witnessed a horrible tragedy. I was reminded of another man who had fallen in the snow—Sigurd F. Olson.

There is such a thing as a fitting death, revolving around time and place, and it seems to me that Sig Olson had one. At the age of eighty-two, he collapsed while out on his snowshoes and died a short time later. It was in January, a season when many old warriors die.

He was a naturalist, educator, writer, and outspoken advocate of the preservation of wilderness. He had spent much of his life in the wild, in many regions of the North American continent, but he considered northern Minnesota his home, especially the border country. He wrote several books about the Quetico-Superior region, the largest wilderness area east of the Rockies. Olson loved this rugged expanse of forests, lakes, and rivers— where timberwolves still hunt, and the aurora borealis cavorts against the stars. Through his writings he was a guide for all who would share his affection.

The Singing Wilderness, Listening Point, Runes of the North, and his other books are enchanting blends of ecology and philosophy. Like Thoreau, Olson believed that people must be able to spend time in the wild in order to fully be themselves. Humans must have a refuge of solitude and tranquility where they can occasionally (or often) escape the turmoil of industrial civilization. Olson wrote of the feeling of "oneness" with the earth and all life that a wilderness trek can generate—the sense of interdependence and bloodlines.

Olson was an environmental activist long before the term was in circulation. As the leader of the National Parks Association and the Wilderness Society, he fought for the Indiana Dunes National Lakeshore on Lake Michigan, the Point Reyes National Seashore in California, Grand Canyon National Park, and the Florida Everglades.

In *Open Horizons* he wrote about what a proposed dam would do to a wild northern river: "The moon was full and the swirling cauldron of currents and foam was a place of magic and mystery, but all I could think of was what would happen should the dam go in, an apron of concrete instead of moonlit surging waves, the great glacial boulder that split the flow above, part of its foundation. The mists might rise again, but the music of that hallowed place would be stilled forever, the enchantment gone."

I heard Olson speak at a symposium on wilderness a few years before he died, and he opened his address with personal tales. Back in the 1920s he had been a guide in the border country. The people he took on fishing trips were often from urban locales such as Chicago or Minneapolis, and he'd see them transformed as they lived day after day in the wild. They became more open, less tense and defensive; they grew attentive to sunsets, trees, and wildlife. A falling leaf or a leaping fish became worthy of comment. But, he added, when it came time to head back to the city, they started hurrying. On the way home they'd revert to the tautness of everyday life. They worried about all the duties and obligations they'd left behind. Olson compared it to the way a horse will run back to its corral when the barn comes into view.

He told of some of the prolonged environmental battles he'd participated in—how he helped prevent the construction of dams in the Boundary Waters Canoe Area Wilderness (BWCAW) and curtailed its use and abuse by aircraft. He suffered a pronounced twitch and his face was deeply creased with age, but his mind was sharp and his voice clear as he expressed his devotion to the lure of the wild country.

The moderator of the symposium had introduced Olson by comparing him to a loon. Sigurd, like a melodious loon, had a cry that we all needed to hear. At that time, in 1978, a bitter conflict was raging over the effort to preserve the BWCAW as a wilderness area. Bills were before Congress that would determine the long-term future of the region. Would it be a haven for wildlife, canoeists, and anglers, or be developed for timber, copper-nickel ore, and snowmobile trails? The legislative alternatives weren't quite that simple, but that's how the battle lines were drawn.

That the BWCAW was threatened was made clear by another speaker on the program. A representative of the timber industry, he arrived at the podium immediately after a standing ovation for Olson. He might have been uncomfortable, but nevertheless he began by offending everyone present. He said he was a native of New York, and in his opinion the BWCAW couldn't "hold a candle to the Adirondacks." Thus bonded to his audience, he developed his main theme: wilderness is a state of mind. He maintained he could know Olson's peace and oneness on a ten-acre woodlot adjacent to a highway and a snow-mobile trail as well as he could in trackless wild lands. He said it wasn't necessary to know that you're twenty miles from the nearest road in order to have a "wilderness feeling."

True. A case can be built for the obvious fact that trees are trees, and a natural setting is a natural setting, and that mere isolation can be irrelevant as far as "communion" is concerned. After all, one can revel in striking sunsets from a skyscraper in downtown Minneapolis. In Sigurd Olson's mind, however, there had to be a place where one could decisively drop out of the modern technological network; a place where you couldn't hear a car, a skidder, or an aircraft; a place where you could be assured you were surrounded by many thousands of acres of untrammeled land, water, and sky. There is a time for isolation. Sometimes it requires a huge mass of quiet before you can hear anything. There must be a sanctuary, a natural archive for the preservation of the ancient states of things. It's a question not only of ecology, biological diversity, and the health of the biosphere, but also of our heritage and the health of our minds. The industry spokesman said he wouldn't be bothered, for example, if some dirt bikes ripped by while he was having a contemplative moment in the woods, but I suspect he was kidding himself. One thing is certain: a white-tailed deer wouldn't be fooled.

As Sigurd Olson wrote in his first book, *The Singing Wilderness,* "What would the wilderness lake country of the Quetico-Superior be like with the roar of motors engulfing it? The charm of a canoe trip is in the quiet as one drifts along the shores, being a part of the rocks and trees and every living thing. How swiftly it changes if all natural sounds are replaced by the explosive violence of combustion engines and speed. At times on quiet waters one does not speak aloud but only in whispers, for then all noise is sacrilege."

In his talk that night Olson conceded that of course we need timber and minerals. But the point is that in all the land mass of the lower forty-eight, only about 3 percent of the acreage is still in a wilderness state, or what we define as such. That leaves 97 percent for us to use and develop (wisely, one hopes). He said: "Surely 3 percent is not too much to ask."

Surely it isn't selfish or wasteful to covet a few million acres out of the two-billion total to keep and preserve for our own peace of mind in a fast, dirty, noisy world. And not only for ourselves, but also for our descendants, and for the sake of the land itself. More than a hundred years ago, when there was a lot more wild country than there is now, Thoreau wrote, "Our village life would stagnate if it were not for the unexplored forests and meadows which surround it. We need the tonic of wildness . . . We can never have enough of nature . . . We need to witness our own limits transgressed and some life pasturing freely where we never wander."

This was also the gospel of Sigurd Olson. He was a prophet in the Old Testament sense of the word. He shared glorious visions and warned us of our follies and their consequences. And as the Bible notes, a prophet has no honor in his own country. At a Congressional hearing concerning the fate of the BWCAW—held in Ely, Minnesota, in July 1978—Sigurd Olson was hung in effigy from the boom of a logging truck. For his readers and supporters, the grotesque dummy bearing his name and twisting in the breeze at the end of a noose was a deeply depressing sight. However, like the ancient prophets, Olson was vindicated in the end, and the Boundary Waters gained protection—at least for a while.

But there are new prophets abroad in the land, men with different visions and new definitions of folly. In their political and economic equations, 3 percent may be too great a sum. Former Interior Secretary James Watt went so far as to invoke the Deity in support of his plans for development. He seemed to view our natural resources in terms of here and now, while people like Olson view a more distant horizon.

Sigurd Olson realized that the struggle for preservation would continue, and he was confident there would be others to take up where he left off. Once, a little more than a year before his death, I had the privilege of speaking to him at his home in Ely. He pointed to a mature Norway pine surrounded by saplings and said, "The big tree is me, I'm about through; but those little ones growing up next to it represent the youth of America. I just toss on the responsibility to youth, and there is the hope of the world . . . there will always be battles."

Then there was the track in the snow, and the place where his snowshoes stopped. And there *are* others to lash on the bindings and continue the trek. The old tree is gone, but saplings are growing.

An Oglala Sioux holy man named Hehaka Sapa said, "The power of the world always works in circles, everything tries to be round."

Thus the growth of trees is measured in rings, and ravens fly circuits over the dead. They will come for me one day. Out of the west, at night.

Peter M. Leschak is a freelance writer who lives in northeastern Minnesota. His work has been published in numerous national and regional periodicals, including *Harper's*, the *New York Times*, *Outdoor Life*, and *Mpls.-St. Paul Magazine*. His previous books are *Letters from Side Lake* (reissued by the University of Minnesota Press in 1992), *Bumming with the Furies*, and *The Bear Guardian*, which won a Minnesota Book Award in 1991. Leschak is also a wildland firefighter, and works fires across the United States for both state and federal agencies. He and his wife, Pam, live in a log house they built on forty acres of forested land.